M

The Reuben/Rifkin Jewish Women Writers Series
A joint project of the Hadassah-Brandeis Institute and The Feminist Press
Series Editors: Elaine Reuben, Shulamit Reinharz, Gloria Jacobs

The Reuben/Rifkin Jewish Women Writers Series, established in 2006 by Elaine Reuben, honors her parents, Albert G. and Sara I. Reuben. It remembers her grandparents, Susie Green and Harry Reuben, Bessie Goldberg and David Rifkin, known to their parents by Yiddish names, and recalls family on several continents, many of whose names and particular stories are now lost. Literary works in this series, embodying and connecting varieties of Jewish experiences, will speak for them, as well, in the years to come.

Founded in 1997, the Hadassah-Brandeis Institute (HBI), whose generous grants also sponsor this series, develops fresh ways of thinking about Jews and gender worldwide by producing and promoting scholarly research and artistic projects. Brandeis professors Shulamit Reinharz and Sylvia Barack Fishman are the founding director and codirector, respectively, of HBI.

Dream Homes

from cairo to katrina, an exile's journey

joyce zonana

The Feminist Press
at The City University of New York
New York

Published in 2008 by The Feminist Press at The City University of New York
The Graduate Center
365 Fifth Avenue, Suite 5406
New York, NY 10016
www.feministpress.org

Library of Congress Cataloging-in-Publication Data

Zonana, Joyce.
Dream homes: from Cairo to Katrina : an exile's journey / Joyce Zonana.
p. cm.
ISBN-13: 978-1-55861-573-1 (trade paper)
ISBN-13: 978-1-55861-574-8 (library)
1. Zonana, Joyce. 2. Zonana, Joyce—Childhood and youth. 3. Jews,
Egyptian—United States—Biography. 4. Jewish women—United States—
Biography. I. Title.
E184.37.Z66 2007
962.004924—dc22
2007033835

Text and cover design by Lisa Force
Printed on acid-free paper in Canada by Transcontinental

12 11 10 09 08   5 4 3 2 1

For Kiana

Contents ◆ ◆ ◆

Acknowledgments ◆ ◆ ◆

As a child, I found my home in books. I dreamed of writing one. But until I began to work on this memoir, I thought of writing as a solitary enterprise. To my surprise, I discovered it to be an intensely communal adventure, bringing me into ever-deepening contact with an ever-widening circle of people. Through the act of writing, I found my home in the world.

This book got its start in the Zora Neale Hurston shed at Norcroft: A Writing Retreat for Women. I was lucky enough to have three luxurious and productive residencies at Norcroft. Two other women's writing retreats also offered me much needed rooms of my own: Hedgebrook and Soapstone. Without the hard work and vision of the women who founded these havens—Joan Drury, Nancy Skinner Nordhoff and Sheryl Feldman, and Judith Barrington and Ruth Gundle, respectively—along with the many others who fund and staff them, I could never have written this book. While at these retreats, I met wonderful women writers whose courage, commitment, and talent inspired and sustained me; among them, Anne Dunn, Susan Freireich, Bushra Rehman, and Cheryl Reitan remain as cherished friends.

In New Orleans, two writing groups provided secure homes for me and my work. One, a supportive circle of women—Gillian Brown, Lynn Byrd, Bonnie Fastring, Alice Kemp, Beverly Rainbolt, and Martha Ward—called itself the Sorta Zona Rosa Group. Meeting monthly to share meals and manuscripts, we took our inspiration from the Zona Rosa groups run by Rosemary Daniell, who also offered her inimitable individual encouragement. The second, a handful of colleagues from the University of New Orleans Department of English, met occasionally for exhilarating afternoon sessions at Joe's Crab Shack on Lake Pontchartrain.

Randolph Bates, John Hazlett, and T. R. Johnson gave my writing the scrupulously detailed critical readings that helped refine my prose and shape the overall manuscript. Joe's is gone, but Randy, John, and T.R. are always with me.

Also in New Orleans, Michele Levy, Christine Murphey, and Darlene Olivo were writing partners and good friends. Kay Murphy loved me and believed in my writing, and she modeled the life of a writer. I cannot thank her enough. My East Coast friends Jimmy Griffin, Laura Rose, and Suzanne Brown read early drafts of the book and shared it with their families. That Jimmy's mother, Laura's father, and Suzanne's husband liked my work kept me going.

Carol Christ gave me the Mediterranean. Mervat Hatem gave me Cairo. Carmen Weinstein gave me Jewish Cairo. The New Orleans Jung Seminar—Battle Bell, Jutta von Buchholtz, Blanche Gelfand, Joan Harrison, Karen Gibson, Mike King, Lucie Magnus, Marilyn Marshall, Charlotte Mathes, Del McNeely, Nancy Qualls-Corbett, Connie Romero, David Schoen, Stephanie Thibodeaux, Deedy Young—gave me my Self. Barbara Koltuv listened.

Florence Howe said, "Yes, I'd like to read it," when, at Martha Ward's insistence, I sent an e-inquiry to The Feminist Press. And then she said, "Yes, we'd like to publish it." In The Feminist Press, I found another extraordinary, unexpected home. Franklin Dennis, Lisa Force, Gloria Jacobs, Jeannette Petras, Anjoli Roy, Janet Tanke . . . everyone I have worked with has been thoughtful, wise, supportive, patient, and smart. Cheers to and for all of you!

My grandmothers and my grandfathers, my mother, my father, my uncles and my aunts, my brother, my cousins, my lovers, my students, my teachers, my friends. Each person I have known has contributed to this book. I thank them all. I thank the spirits of all the directions. And, most of all, I thank the Great Spirit.

One: Heirloom ♦ ♦ ♦

*Deep inside, we know we'll lose
everything we own at least twice in our lives.*
—André Aciman, *Out of Egypt*

For many years, my lover slept in her maternal grandmother's bed, an antique mahogany four-poster, high off the ground, with an arching, inlaid headboard. During the year we lived together in my tiny New Orleans home, Kay stored the bed, along with its matching dresser and vanity, in a damp

Suleiman Pasha square, Cairo, 1906. Courtesy of Max Karkegi, *L'Egypte d'Antan* (www.egyptedantan.com/egypt.htm).

commercial warehouse, where it languished, threatened by decay. My mattress was too wide, and the house was already too crowded. But Kay yearned for her grandmother's bed; without it, her sleep was disturbed. She and her grandmother had been each other's favorites. As a child, Kay found peace at her grandmother's side; later, she nursed her during her final illness. When her grandmother died, the family urged Kay to take what she wanted. Along with the bedroom suite, she chose bookshelves, end tables, a heavy chest of drawers—all in that dark mahogany, carved and rich with detail. She transported it from Illinois in a rented van, driving the long miles with the help of a friend.

When we moved together to a larger house near Bayou St. John, Kay arranged the worn wood around her. When I hesitated to place a cup of coffee on an end table, she reassured me. "Don't worry, my grandmother always put bottles of Coke there. If it was OK for my grandmother, it's OK for us."

The table was marked by years of wear, with scratches and ring-marks, the faded veneer warped and cracked. Yet it shone with the warmth of age. I tried to imagine what it might be like to live surrounded by objects that belonged to one's grandmother, objects that furnished the world of one's birth, creating by their contours the texture of memory. For most of my life, I have been baffled by the American passion for antiques, the delight taken in the heavy, cumbersome pieces that filled the farmhouses and prairie homes of my friends' ancestors. My taste has tended toward bare, unfinished simplicity—utilitarian furniture one can assemble and disassemble with ease, interchangeable, spare parts that resist attachment, repel nostalgia. Watching Kay dust and oil her battered treasures, I began to understand.

"What wealth you have, what a great inheritance," I told her. Her protests failed to move me. Even when she reminded me that her parents' four-room house in Illinois had only an outdoor toilet and was covered with tar paper, I remained convinced of her wealth. "You have your grandmother's things."

◆

My own grandmothers were left behind in Cairo in 1951 when my parents, Egyptian Jews, brought me, eighteen months old, on a boat to the United States. They didn't carry much—a little money, clothes, linens, some silver trays and prayer rugs—nothing that couldn't be squeezed into a few worn suitcases. Although they had waited five years for the visa granting them entrance to the United States, they didn't want the officials in Cairo to suspect them of planning to emigrate. They were slipping away quietly, taking with them only what they could carry, trying to make it look as if they were simply taking a short vacation in Italy. Silver trays? Prayer rugs? Gold jewelry? For a brief vacation? Apparently the customs officer let these pass. Left behind, though, were the bed and dresser crafted for them when they married, the dining table and chairs my father had known since infancy. Because they reasoned that no one would think to examine an eighteen-month-old child, I served as the bearer of the family legacy: Dressed in several layers of clothing, I was decked with the additional jewels my parents thought the customs officer might balk at. I wore rings, necklaces, bracelets, pins—anything they could manage to secure on me. They were of gold and silver, embellished with turquoise, rubies, and tiny seed pearls; among them were a filigreed gold *khamsa* to ward off the evil eye; an eighteen-carat gold mesh bracelet in the form of a snake; silver mezuzahs; enameled brooches; and a pale gold locket, heart shaped, etched with flowers.

I know this not because I remember but because I have been told, because I have listened avidly to the few words my parents have let drop about this voyage. Much as I would like to, I remember nothing of the boat, nothing of my infant days in Cairo, not much even of the first years in New York. And my parents—Felix was thirty-six, Nelly thirty, when they left their home—have been reluctant to talk about it. They appear to suffer from a kind of amnesia, an involuntary—or is it willed?—

failure to recollect. Obsessively, I ask questions, but I obtain only fragments, bits and pieces I painstakingly arrange and rearrange in my effort to grasp the whole. "What was it like?" I plead. "How did it feel?" "What did you think?" The answers I receive are fixed, rigid, laconic: a few details, ritually repeated, like verses of an ancient prayer; rough, unsanded boards—nothing like even the most rudimentary chair or table where I might sit, dream, feed my imagination.

◆

The year was 1951, the boat the *Fiorello La Guardia*, our destination New York City. The trip lasted twenty-one days.

"*Tu étais très malade*," my mother tells me. "You were very sick. You had a high fever, and they told us we had to stay in our room."

"We were quarantined?" The idea is exotic, simultaneously romantic and frightening, evoking scenes of turn-of-the-century immigration, the long lines and cold examination rooms at Ellis Island. Where were we? On the boat? In New York Harbor? My mother's focus drifts.

"Yes, quarantined," she repeats. "That's the word. *On était si bête*. We were so stupid. I stayed with you in the hotel for three days while Felix went out. No one ever checked."

"We were in a hotel? You mean the boat was docked?" I ask, struggling for precision. "Where were we?"

"Yes," my mother replies, returning from her reverie. "The boat was docked in Naples." By then, the pretense of the short Italian vacation had been abandoned. We were on our way to New York. "I wanted to see the city," my mother continues, "but they said I had to stay in the room. We were so stupid. We didn't know anything. On the boat they brought me tea in little bags, and I had never seen anything like that before. I opened the bags and put the tea leaves in the cup. *J'étais si bête*. I was so stupid. They must have been laughing at me."

Part of the reason she can't remember, I suddenly realize,

must be because she is embarrassed, ashamed of her ignorance. It is a trait we share. Living in what still often feels to me like an alien land, I retain her fear of saying or doing the wrong thing, letting slip a word or a gesture that will betray me, revealing my foreignness. Like her, I call myself "stupid"—*bête*—worry, stay silent.

"Not stupid," I try to reassure her, "you just didn't know."

My mother tells me she was seasick for the entire voyage, remaining below deck, vomiting, drinking black tea littered with leaves.

"Don't you remember anything else?" I persist. "What was the ocean like?"

"I went out only once," she eventually concedes, "at Gibraltar. I remember the sky, the stars. There were—how do you say it?—*falaises*, like in England—big cliffs—on both sides. It was very beautiful."

I picture a young woman, traveling with her husband and child, leaving behind parents, siblings, cousins, friends. She is alone and frightened, barely able to stand. Perhaps her husband tells her they are about to pass the Straits of Gibraltar. She has studied geography at the lycée in Cairo, knows where this is. She climbs up to the deck, holds her husband's arm, breathes deeply of the night air, takes her last look at the Mediterranean. The *Fiorello La Guardia* steams out into the Atlantic, as my mother succumbs once more to vertigo.

◆

Five, six, seven years later, in our meticulously kept kitchen in Brooklyn, my mother sings, encouraging me to eat:

> "*Il était un petit navire,*
> *Il était un petit navire,*
> *Qui n'avait ja-ja-jamais navigué*
> *Qui n'avait ja-ja-jamais navigué*
> *O-wais-o-wais-o-wais. . . .*"

The song describes the adventures of a young sailor on his first ocean voyage, a trip across the Mediterranean:

> *"Sur la mer-mer-mer Méditerranée*
> *Sur la mer-mer-mer Méditerranée*
> *Sur la mer-mer-mer Méditerranée*
> *O-wais-o wais-o wais. . . ."*

After several weeks at sea, the ship is becalmed, and food supplies are exhausted. The starving sailors draw lots to determine who will be eaten. The *petit navire*, the song's young hero, is chosen. Moments before he is to be sacrificed, a landward wind arises and the ship sails safely to port.

I loved this macabre little song, with its cheerfully matter-of-fact threat of cannibalism, and I would often deliberately not eat, just to hear it again. While my mother sang, I dreamed of the *Méditerranée*, that mysterious blue sea she evoked with such love—the sea where innocent sailors might be eaten without remorse, the sea that glittered in her memory, forever shining on the other side of Gibraltar.

"What was it like," I ask, "to leave everybody behind in Cairo? Did *Nonna* and *Nonno* come to the dock to see you off?" My mother cannot answer, turns away, tells me that *Tante* Suze and *Oncle* Joe—my Aunt Suze and Uncle Joe—met us in New York. "But what was it like in Cairo?" I ask again, "Who came to the dock?" My mother remains silent, doesn't even tell me that the ship left from Alexandria, not Cairo.

I recall a moment several years back at one of the large train stations in Prague. Kay and I had spent a weekend in the city, and now she was leaving to return to Austria, while I was to remain in the Czech Republic for another week. Her train left early, and I accompanied her to the crowded station before dawn. Together we walked along the echoing platform to her carriage, located her compartment and her seat, put up her luggage. I said good-bye, then stood outside, watching the long train pull away. We waved, blew kisses, laughed as I pretended to cry.

But as the train receded into the brown countryside, I was surprised by the real tears that suddenly burned my face. Within moments I was sobbing, my shoulders convulsed. Embarrassed, I tried to stop myself. These tears made no sense. Kay and I would be separated for less than a week; we would be seeing one another before long. Yet I was inconsolable. Alone on that empty platform in a city where I could not speak the language, I sank into the pain of my first departure, the pain that awaits me at every good-bye. It is the memory I do not have, the experience that shapes all memory. The boat sails; the train pulls away. I hear the echoing blast of the steamship, the receding cry of the train. And I do not know if I am the one left behind or if I am the one leaving, if I am the one on the dock or on the ship, the platform or the train. What I know are the tears, the loss, the terrified certainty that I will never again see the loved face.

I decide to stop badgering my mother.

◆

My mother's parents—*Nonna* and *Nonno*, Allegra and Selim Chalom—came to New York in 1956, five years after we had left Cairo. My father and *Oncle* Joe had tried for many years to obtain entry visas for them, but U.S. immigration quotas admitted only one hundred Egyptians a year. In Egypt most Jews were not regarded as citizens. Some had passports from European nations, and many were simply stateless, *apatride*. Yet from the point of view of U.S. immigration, they were Egyptians. During the Suez Crisis—when Britain, France, and Israel attacked Egypt after Nasser nationalized the Suez Canal— more than twenty thousand Jews either fled or were expelled from the country. Although the United States did not classify them as political refugees, some managed to enter the States; most emigrated to Israel or to Latin America. Along with *Tante*

Diane, and my *Oncles* Albert, Lucien, and Eli, my maternal grandparents were moving to Brazil, where they would settle in São Paulo.

My mother, my two-year-old brother, Victor, and I drove to Idlewild Airport in the used Mercury my parents had just bought. At the age of seven, I already knew the airport well. We would go whenever a relative came to visit, and relatives were always visiting, strange men and elaborately made-up women who slept on the living room couch and talked loudly in French and Arabic, greeting me with astonished comments about how much I had grown, how closely I resembled my mother and grandmother. In time, my parents discovered that a trip to the airport could be as entertaining as a picnic at the Cloisters or a stroll through the Brooklyn Botanical Gardens. We would park the car in a large outdoor lot, then walk to the observation tower, where we spent happy hours watching planes taking off and landing.

But this trip to the airport was not an excursion. My mother was on edge, anxious. Her parents were arriving, and though I had no conscious memory of them, I had been told that they loved me, that they would be happy to see me again. From photographs I knew that my grandfather wore a soft Fedora and that my grandmother's white hair fell in thin strands from a loose bun; they were both stooped, with rounded shoulders and bent necks. We were to meet them at the International Arrivals Building, after they passed through customs, "*la douane.*" *La douane.* The words were ominous, frightening, uttered always with a kind of hushed respect. I sensed that they referred to a mystery one could not fathom, a force one could not control. What would the officials do? What would they find? Could they turn one back? I worried for my unknown grandparents who would have to go through *la douane.*

◆

In the mid-1950s the customs area at Idlewild was in a huge rectangular room at the center of the International Arrivals

Building. People awaiting family or visitors from abroad could look down from a glassed-in gallery high above the bare white room. When we learned that my grandparents' plane had landed, my mother and brother and I made our way to that gallery, watching the hundreds of people slowly moving through *la douane*.

"How will we recognize them?" I asked my mother. "How will we know who they are? Will they know we're here?"

The crowd seemed huge, a dull mass of solemn adults in heavy coats and hats. My mother was eager, holding my hand tightly, ceaselessly scanning the room below.

Then suddenly she pointed. *"Là. Ils sont là. Là. Regarde!"*

And she started banging against the glass, waving, jumping. *"Maman! Papa! Maman!"* She hurried us down the corridor so that we would be standing directly in front of the line where my grandparents waited, holding their passports, not even knowing to look up.

"Maman! Papa!" she continued to cry, banging the glass. I was self-conscious, not wanting her to call attention to our family. But of course that's exactly what my mother was intending to do. Call attention to us, get her mother and father to see us all. In those days, I hated to be out with my mother in public. There she would be, obviously attached to me, speaking in her awkward, accented English, asking questions that embarrassed me, acting so unmistakably foreign, while I ached to be like everyone else. But here everyone else was also banging on the glass, waving, trying to attract the attention of disoriented relatives stumbling across this last hurdle before the embrace of arrival.

Eventually, *Nonna* and *Nonno* looked up; they must have noticed others doing it, glimpsed the broad smiles illuminating otherwise bewildered faces. It was *Nonno* who saw us first, and he bent gently toward his wife, taking her hand, pointing upwards, showing her Nelly, Nelly and the children. Allegra smiled, burst into tears. My mother waved with both hands, her body pressed against the glass. She held my young brother up so they could see him, pulled me in front of her proudly.

And then we waited, waited and watched and worried as we saw the customs man order them to open their bags, to undo carefully wrapped packages, to answer questions. I could see the man my mother called Papa, whom I was to call *Nonno*. He was shaking his head, spreading his hands in a gesture that seemed to say, "I'm sorry, this is the best I can do."

"Do they speak any English?" I asked my mother.

"*Non*," she replied, "*Ils ne* speak *pas* English."

"Shouldn't we help them?" I wondered. I wanted to run down to these old people trapped behind that glass wall, unable to speak the language, lost. I wanted to take their hands, to talk to the customs officer in my perfect, unaccented English, to lead them proudly from the chaos of the airport to the order of our small apartment in the Shore Haven housing complex. I still see them there, *Nonna* and *Nonno*, bewildered in that huge room at Idlewild, speechless and alone; I still want to go to them, to take them home with me, introduce them to the United States, our home. Of their visit itself—did my grandmother hold me? did my grandfather smile?—I, like my mother, have no memory. I only know that, after a month, *Nonna* and *Nonno* left us, moving to Brazil with my *Tante* Diane and *Oncles* Albert, Lucien, and Eli.

◆

On the *Fiorello La Guardia*, because my mother was sick in the second-class cabin, I was out every day with my father, as he paced the deck. I like to think that sometimes he held me, lifting me in his arms so that I might look over the rails.

"What was it like?" I begged him to tell me in the years before his death. "What did we do all day? How did you feel?"

My mother would answer for him. "He was nervous. Your father had never spent any time with you before, and he was nervous. He didn't know what to do with you."

And I would turn again to my father, "What was it like? How did you feel?"

"I was scared," he would finally say, emerging with difficulty from the rigidity of advanced Parkinson's disease. "I was very nervous. We didn't know what we were going to find. I didn't know what I was going to do. I was scared."

In Cairo, my father—who had earned a French law degree—held a job as an interpreter of French and Arabic in the Mixed Courts. The courts, established in 1875, had jurisdiction over civil disputes between foreigners—among whom many Jews were counted—and Egyptians. Most Jewish men in Cairo worked in business and the professions, often as textile merchants or bankers, but my father cherished the security and prestige of his civil service appointment, as well as his status as an Egyptian citizen. Working for the Egyptian government, he would have a pension, the guarantee of a lifetime job. It was not something he could have given up easily.

"So why did you decide to leave?" I continued to probe.

"J'ai vu l'écriture sur le mur," he whispered, pointing a trembling finger and opening his eyes wide, as if to show me the crumbling wall he could still see, inscribed with anti-Semitic comments. "I saw the writing on the wall. I could see what was coming." He was pleased with himself, proud of his prophetic acumen, yet annoyed with my question. I shouldn't have to ask.

During and after World War II, in addition to working in the Mixed Courts, my father served as social secretary for Haim Nahum Effendi, the Chief Rabbi of Cairo. An esteemed scholar and astute diplomat, the Chief Rabbi worked to defuse the developing tensions between Jews and Arabs, refusing to identify himself—and the larger Sephardic Jewish community he represented—with either extreme Zionism or radical Egyptian nationalism. I imagine the rabbi talking with my father about the mounting signs that Jews might no longer be welcome in Egypt; I wonder if he didn't encourage my father to make his plans to leave.

"He was a great man," my father said of the Chief Rabbi. "He always worked for peace."

My mother interjects: "We have a card from him; he gave us a card," and she rummages through a box of old papers and photos until she finds it, the engraved calling card signed with flourishes by Cairo's Chief Rabbi, wishing "*chères Félix et Nelly bonne chance*" in the United States.

My father made his decision to emigrate early in 1946, a year after he married my mother and a few months after the terrible Cairo riots that erupted on November 2 and 3, 1945, the anniversary of the 1917 Balfour Declaration promising the establishment of a Jewish homeland in Palestine. Members of Young Egypt and the Muslim Brotherhood transformed what was to have been a peaceful anti-Zionist demonstration into an anti-Jewish riot. The Ashkenazi synagogue on al-Noubi Street was pillaged and set ablaze, Jewish-owned department stores in the elegant downtown were looted, and shouts of "Down with the Jews, down with colonization," echoed through the streets of the city. On the second day of the riots, Jewish shops on my grandparents' street were stoned.

My father's older brother applied for a visa a month after my father did; although our chance to emigrate came in 1951, my uncle's visa was not granted until late in 1956. In the month between the two brothers' applications, hundreds, perhaps thousands, of Jews must have been making the difficult decision to leave the nation where they had prospered for more than half a century.

Even during World War II—with the exception of the days when Rommel's troops threatened Alexandria—the more than eighty thousand Jews of Egypt had lived well. "We didn't care about a thing," a relative once told me. "We had our heads in the sand. Life was good." But in 1945 and 1946, emerging Egyptian nationalism, coupled with sympathy for Palestinian Arabs who were about to lose *their* homeland, triggered attacks against Jews, who were suspected of Zionism and of identifying with the British occupiers of Egypt. In the years after 1946, attacks against Jews increased, culminating in seizures of property, arrests, and, finally, expulsions.

I consider how, until his death, my father worried about our family's safety and security. "Explain to me," he often asked, "tell me what tenure means. Does it mean you can't lose your job?"

"Yes," I would assure him, "I can keep this job as long as I want." I was an associate professor in the English Department of the University of New Orleans, the city's major public university. After a long probation, I had acquired what few people in the United States have—a permanent, full-time, relatively well paying, and, best of all, extremely fulfilling job.

"Good," my father would say, comforted. "But don't do anything to make them upset with you."

My father was convinced that one cannot be too careful. Haunted by a keen sense of the fragility of social life, he knew that one could be jettisoned at a moment's notice, one's livelihood gone, one's standing lost. With alarming regularity, he asked me how much I made, if I was saving for retirement, if I got along with my neighbors and colleagues. When I moved to Oklahoma for my first teaching job, he had worried. "Do they know about Jews there? Will you be safe?"

My father's fears may have been a legacy from childhood. His own father died suddenly when he was four, and his mother, alone with three boys, was forced to turn to her widowed mother and mother-in-law for help. In that financially strained household with no adult men, my father, the sensitive middle son, would have imbibed the women's anxious determination to act *comme il faut*—as one must—in order to maintain their hold on middle-class respectability. He grew to be a cautious man troubled by a concern for order, propriety, the opinions of others. Yet sometimes I think his anxieties should be attributed to the collective traumas of World War II and its aftermath rather than to individual family psychology. He never forgot those days before

Al-Alamein, when Rommel's forces were poised to overtake Alexandria, and Jews throughout Egypt feared the worst; he always remembered how, during the 1948 war with Israel, while my mother was pregnant with me, he was arrested, imprisoned, and interrogated by Egyptian soldiers who suspected him of having constructed a bomb in the family's apartment kitchen.

I struggle to picture this timid, delicate man—at the end nearly paralyzed with Parkinson's disease—pacing the decks of the *Fiorello La Guardia*, holding my small hand, seeking answers to what I'm sure even then were my incessant, though barely articulate, questions. "Where are we going?" "Why?" "When will we get there?" He had no job, no prospects. A man reliant on his ability to follow rules precisely, he was entering a country where he did not know the rules, where he would be forced to find his way without coordinates. When, in elementary school, I was introduced to graph paper, I would spend hours carefully drawing objects to scale. Later, I became fascinated with the use of the x and y axes to chart points. On a road trip, no matter who is driving, I appoint myself navigator. I pore over maps, plan routes, check constantly to see if we have reached the markers indicated in the guidebooks. I am my father's daughter. I need always to know where I am. Like him, I fear the horrible free fall of being lost, at sea.

◆

I have inherited neither antique furniture nor an ancestral home. I do not have a grandmother's house. What I have instead are fragments of stories and tiny pieces of moveable property—what Wemmick, in *Great Expectations*, advises Pip to get his hands on—that made the journey with my parents from Cairo. Jewelry, embroidery, books, silver: These are my heirlooms, my relics of the past. On my wall is a delicate needlepoint canvas depicting sailboats—feluccas—at sunset on the Nile; in my cupboard are engraved silver trays that once adorned my grandmother's table; and although it is much battered, I still have one of the beautifully woven prayer rugs my mother received at her wedding. Jewish peoples, I remind myself, rarely owned land; they invested whatever wealth they could amass in precious objects that moved quietly from hand to hand. Small things, nearly invisible—certainly unnoticeable to those who do not know what to look for. A migratory people, my ancestors learned to love what they could carry, and to carry what they loved.

I remember a gold locket that belonged to my maternal grandmother: eighteen karat, heart shaped, with delicate roses etched on its face. One summer evening in New York I sat with a friend at dusk on a bench in Central Park, talking after a pleasant dinner, prolonging our time together. The locket was on my neck, cool against my sun-warmed skin. A man approached us, asking for a match. When I said I didn't have one, he stepped back, then lunged suddenly toward me, with a knife I thought, directed at my throat. What he wanted, I realized too late, was the locket, glinting in the fading light. His hand grasped it, twisted the chain, and wrenched it from me as he jumped away, into the bushes across from us and out into the street. Stunned, I clutched my throat, and began to cry with grief and rage. He could not have known what it meant to me, this tiny piece of worked gold. What would it bring in a pawn shop? Surely not its worth. My grandmother's locket. What stories does it hold?

Two: Chez Les Arabes   ◆ ◆ ◆

It is a bright Saturday afternoon, crisp fall weather outside, and I am in my small New Orleans kitchen, preparing stuffed grape leaves for the annual department party. My task began

Joyce and Nelly Zonana at a Brooklyn Farmer's Market, 2007. Courtesy of Kathy Asbury.

late last night, when I rinsed a cup of chickpeas and placed them in a bowl, covering them with fresh spring water. This morning, I peeled the chickpeas one by one, rubbing each swollen kernel between my palms until the dull skin slipped off to reveal the bright yellow core, plumply wrinkled, like an ancient stone goddess. Now, while the beans simmer, I mince four yellow onions, a head of garlic, two bunches of parsley, six tomatoes. My worn wooden cutting board is soaked in red juice, stained a deep green. In a large glass bowl, I combine the onions, garlic, tomatoes, and parsley with raw white rice, freshly squeezed lemon juice, olive oil, allspice. When they are tender, I add the warm, just-cooked chickpeas.

The filling for my grape leaves is ready at last; time now to "stuff." With deliberation, I spread a vine leaf—veined side up—on a plate, snip off its stem with my thumbnail, and place a spoonful of the rice mixture at its base. With both hands, I fold in the leaf's sides; then, keeping the folds in place with my right hand, I roll with my left, working to create a tight, narrow cylinder. I have two pounds of grape leaves to prepare in this manner—perhaps a hundred, two hundred leaves; I always lose track. As I complete each little packet, pressing firmly to seal it, I place it in the cast-iron pot where it will simmer for an hour, fitted snugly in even rows beneath a plate weighted with stones.

"Never again," I say to myself. "Never again."

The skin on my fingers is puckered and raw; my back hurts, my eyes burn, and the music I put on earlier has begun to cloy. I am tired, bored with my task. A few hours ago it was absorbing, but my interest has waned. I wonder, When will I be done? Will I have time to clean the kitchen, shower, relax before the party? Will I have a chance to read, work on my *Jane Eyre* essay? I lose my focus and the leaf I am rolling loses its shape. Bits of rice and onion and tomato stick out from the sides. I undo the cylinder, absently chew the leaf, lick the tart, sweet juice from my fingers. I am thinking about Jane, her ambition and desire. The next leaf tears as I peel it from the stack. I cannot use it.

Abruptly, angry with myself, I bring myself back. Slowing my pace and concentrating, I separate the next leaf from the stack, laying it gently on the plate, using both hands. I fill a tablespoon with the rice mixture.

Hours later, once they have cooked and are cooled to room temperature, I arrange the dark green rolls, piling them high onto silver trays, garnishing them with lemon slices, tomato wedges, black olives. I bring these trays to the party, place them on the table beside bowls of chips, raw vegetables, sour cream dip. Maybe no one will eat them, I think, and I'll be able to take some home, rationing them to myself for lunch and dinner during the week. But, no, I'm not that lucky. At the end of the evening, my platters are empty, though there are still chips and dips in the bowls beside them. A few colleagues comment on my creation. "Delicious," they remark, "really delicious."

"Never again," I say to myself. "Never again."

Still, six months later, I hear the words come out of my mouth, as I stand in a group planning a party.

"I'll make grape leaves," I say. "I'll bring stuffed grape leaves."

And again, as if in a daze, sleepwalking, I take myself to the Palestinian grocery store not far from my home. I buy dried chickpeas, allspice, wide jars of leaves preserved in brine. These jars, imported from Greece or Lebanon or Turkey, are sealed with hermetic force: I have to bang and twist and coax their lids off, then slip cautious fingers below their narrow necks to pry out the thick packets of leaves.

◆

When I lived in Oklahoma, I would pick leaves right off the vines that covered my back fence. Cooked, their flavor was pungent, sharp. Here in New Orleans, the local health food store occasionally carries fresh leaves. When I see them, I don't even ask the price—I buy whatever is available, set chickpeas to soaking, chop onions and tomatoes. As I work I dream of all the vineyards across the globe—in Greece, in Italy, in California, New York. Rows and rows of grape leaves. What happens to all those leaves, I wonder: Are they all brought to market? Why am I the only woman I know who is compelled to buy and cook them?

◆

My mother made stuffed grape leaves at least once a month. She used beef, not chickpeas, and so she was spared the soaking and peeling that take so much of my time. But she rolled her leaves more tightly, making tiny, narrow cylinders. We ate the trim delicacies greedily, unconscious of the effort enfolded in each. My mother didn't mind, she encouraged our greed, offering "more," "more," "have some more." Along with the grape leaves she served *fila au fromage*, small baked pastries of crisp phyllo dough wrapped around a tangy filling of Parmesan and feta cheese; and *kobéba*, deep-fried, crunchy bulgur dumplings stuffed with chopped beef and pine nuts, flavored with pomegranate syrup. This wasn't the main meal, just the appetizers, *les mézzés*, which also included homemade pickled vegetables—turnip, artichoke, lemon, or cauliflower marinated in brine or vinegar—along with *tahina*, pita bread, and—for those concerned about calories— unadorned raw slivers of carrots and celery.

Cooking was my mother's passion, the force that led her, guiding her choices. If we couldn't have the whole of the life she had left behind in Cairo in 1951—if we couldn't have the heavy wooden furniture that filled her parents' apartment on the rue Suleiman Pasha, or the blue sky over the Nile, or the sounds and smells of Groppi's, or the silent majesty of the pyramids guarding the desert, or her mother and father themselves, her sisters and brothers and cousins—we would have the food, all the food, in all its complex, abundant, aromatic intricacy. In Cairo, there had been servants and relatives and friends to help prepare the elaborate dishes. In Brooklyn, my mother labored without assistance to produce *bamyia, loubia, m'ggadereh, cousa be gebna, hamoud, kobéba*. Alone in our narrow apartment kitchen, she chopped and peeled and simmered and stewed, shelling pounds of beans, trimming hundreds of artichokes, spreading what must have been, over the years, acres of fine phyllo dough. Her strong large hands were red, rubbed raw from repeated immersions in water, prolonged contact with the skins of acidic fruits and vegetables. And they were covered with blisters, large puckered blisters that seemed never to heal: She persistently burned herself, picking up skillets with bare hands, letting hot oil sputter onto fingers and wrists.

Long before every holiday meal—and there were dozens, it seemed, each year throughout my childhood, bright havens of warmth that marked the seasons of Jewish life—she would begin to formulate a menu, balancing the requirements of tradition against the vagaries of the market. At each festival she would serve seven or eight dishes, along with the carefully prepared ritual foods—deep red pomegranates and quince jelly for Rosh Hashanah; date-filled, wine-soaked *charoseth* and an airy, unleavened nut cake for Pesach; honey-dipped *beignets* to break the fast on Yom Kippur. On ordinary nights as well, we had an abundance of selections. My mother's offerings were gloriously varied—never the spare balance of meat and potatoes—but always the generous harmonies of rice and lentils simmered with onions and topped with yogurt; a salad of lettuce and tomatoes seasoned with cumin and fresh lemon juice; a shimmering cornstarch pudding scented with rosewater and studded with pistachios. Tomatoes and zucchini were stuffed with rice or beef; dried apricots and prunes were soaked and stewed with chicken; phyllo dough was brushed with butter, filled with cheese or spinach or ground meat, then baked until crisp. Cooking was my mother's art, her sacrament. She dreamed food, lived it, even as today I dream words, seeking sustenance.

"Eat," my mother says, hovering anxiously between stove and table. "Eat. Do you want more?"

"Read," I beg my friends, as I place a manuscript before them. "Read. Do you want to see more?"

For several years now, I have been piecing together this memoir, assembling the fragments of my story and the story of my family, attempting to roll them together into tidy packets, letting them simmer in the juice of imagination. Language, I like to think, will make *my* past present, bringing continuity and coherence to a life marked by loss. I write to tell my story, though I wonder if my American English words have the savor of *kamoun* and *kuzbara* and *buhar*. Will my grape leaves keep their shape, or will the packets come undone, leaving more bits and pieces scattered about?

◆

We ate well in our Brooklyn home, but we ate differently. Our neighbors were Irish, Italian, and Jewish. But the Jews were Ashkenazi, Eastern Europeans with ancestors from Russia and Poland and Germany or Austria-Hungary—nothing like our Mediterranean tribe. With the exception of my father's cousin Sheila, who arrived from Cairo with her family in 1960, there was no one else in all of Shore Haven (and it was a huge housing complex, with some twenty buildings, each six stories high, eight apartments to a floor) who ate as we did. I savored the complex aromas of marinara sauce for meatballs and spaghetti served by the Italian families who lived above and beside and below us, and I longed to eat as they did, but I was not puzzled by the differences in our foodways. We were Egyptian and Jewish. They were Italian and Catholic. That explained things. But what about the other Jews? I had difficulty understanding our culinary divergence. And for them it was even more difficult.

"You mean you're Jewish? And you don't know about gefilte fish?"

This from my best friend Debbie's mother, who, on Friday nights, cooked chicken soup, kugel, kishke, latkes—a tempting array of textures, colors, and scents. I begged permission to visit the Saltzes' apartment, just across the courtyard from ours, so that I might enjoy the pleasures of their Sabbath kitchen. The

Saltzes kept kosher; they had separate plates for meat and dairy, as well as a special set of glass dishes for Passover. Debbie taught me to distinguish among the sets, warning me never to put dairy on a meat dish. And she explained, to my puzzlement, that fish could be *either* dairy or meat. All the Jews in the neighborhood kept kosher, it seemed, except us. When I asked my mother why we didn't, she said it wasn't important: "What difference does it make?" But I knew the difference it made. Real Jews kept kosher—that was how one could tell they were Jewish. Much as I enjoyed our tabbouleh and *hamoud*, I believed that if we were really Jewish, we would be eating stuffed cabbage, not stuffed grape leaves. I wanted to stand in line at the corner deli with everyone else on Sunday mornings, to take my number in the busy store loud with good-natured kibbitzing, to order bagels, cream cheese, lox, whitefish. Instead we had *ful medammes* and *tahina*, served with a wilted salad in warm pita bread.

"What kind of a Jew are you?" a schoolmate would challenge during recess.

"Sephardic," I would say, "I'm Sephardic." Although I had no concept of the word's meaning, I knew it was the right one. Our kind was Sephardic; the others were Ashkenazi. "We're from Egypt," I would assert boldly.

"But all the Jews left Egypt a long time ago, isn't that what Passover is about?"

"No," I would say, having been taught the words by my father. "Some Jews went back when they got kicked out of Spain. The Jews did very well in Egypt."

"There are no Jews in Egypt," my little friend would retort. "I never heard of any Jews in Egypt. You can't be Jewish."

It was puzzling, I knew, but I could find nothing further to say at this point. Aside from a handful of relatives, I didn't know any other Jews from Egypt either. An Egyptian Jew. To my neighbors, it seemed an exotic contradiction in terms. To me as well. What was the Egyptian part, what the Jewish? How did they fit together? Maybe I wasn't really Jewish.

"Egyptian, wow. I never met an Egyptian before. Does that mean you're related to Cleopatra?"

That was another question. Was I? It didn't seem likely. But in what way was I Egyptian, then? I knew nothing about Egypt or Egyptians, except the occasional anecdote my parents let slip. I had been told that I was born in Cairo, that my mother took me to the Pyramids at Giza when I was an infant, that I learned to swim at Ras al-Bar, a sand bar in the Nile delta.

"Did you live in a pyramid?"

"Did you ride a camel?"

"Did your mother wear a veil?"

The questions would come, faster and faster, and I could answer none of them. I was a mystery to myself, confused and ashamed. My parents told me I was both Egyptian and Jewish, but on those Brooklyn streets, I could be sure of neither. The two identities threatened to cancel each other; I feared I had no authentic claim to one or the other. Baffled, stymied, I retreated into our apartment, found my way to the kitchen, asked my mother for some *halawah*.

◆

My mother bought the fruits and vegetables that were the core of our meals at the open-air Italian market that lined the sidewalks below the elevated "subway" on Eighty-sixth Street—the old West End line that ran from the tall brick buildings on Fifty-seventh Street in Manhattan to the sweeping boardwalks and wide beaches of Coney Island. Before I was old enough for school, and later, on Saturdays, I would accompany my mother, walking the long blocks in rhythm with the clattering wheels of the shopping cart she pulled behind her.

Each week, my mother and I browsed the full length of the market street, some five or six blocks, before deciding which vegetables to buy. My mother would resist all attempts to entrap her prematurely; she would inspect everything before making a choice, carefully comparing price, quality, and size—looking for the perfectly balanced buy, the most for her money. Taking her time, she would fill brown paper bags with her individually chosen selections—small artichokes, bright green and compact; tender black-eyed peas, barely sprung from the vine; and tiny okra, firm and fresh.

"Lady, you're going to drive away all my customers," an irritated greengrocer would say.

Initially impatient, in time the vendors came to respect my mother, setting aside the finest produce only she could appreciate.

"I have something I think you'll like, Mrs. Zonana," they would call out, as we began our survey of the street. "Look, isn't this beautiful?" "I don't know," my mother would reply, noncommittal. We continued in our usual manner to the end of the market, stopping on the way back only if we had found nothing better. Painstakingly, then, my mother would count her coins (she still did her numbers in French, translating every sum), pulling a needlepoint purse from between her breasts.

◆

I loved these trips to Eighty-sixth Street with my mother, partly because I loved being out, released from the intensity of our small apartment, and partly because I was entranced by the variety and abundance of the vegetables, the busy life of the street. Once home, though, I lost all interest in the food we had amassed. The adventure was over and I refused to participate any further: I would not help my mother in the kitchen. Before the age of seven I had determined I would never be a wife, and I stubbornly resisted my mother's efforts to pass on her skills. Dusting, vacuuming, ironing—I could not avoid these household chores. But cooking, I refused. I would not, I told myself, become a housewife. I wanted freedom, an unscripted life in the larger terrain of the New World that beckoned beyond our immigrant home. Doggedly, I turned to books, imagining they might open the path into my future—away from our family's largely unspoken but evidently painful, and, to me, constricting, past.

My desk and my notebooks, then, took the place of my mother's stove and mixing bowls, words substituting for vegetables and spices. Like the kitchen cabinets crammed with jars of beans and grains, the shelf above my bed overflowed with dictionaries and encyclopedias. I spent hours examining etymologies, pronunciations, meanings. As my mother compared artichokes on Eighty-sixth Street, squeezing them between her fingers and bringing them to her nose, I evaluated synonyms in my bedroom, rifling through an old thesaurus, sampling the sounds: "Hunger," I said to myself, "appetite, craving, greed." "Identity," I pondered, "agreement, likeness, self."

Bilingual in French and English by the age of two, I seemed to know from the start that some things could be said only in one language, that translations were always approximate. "*Il n'y a pas de quoi*," we said graciously in French, while Americans muttered a bare "You're welcome"; "*Comme il faut*," we said to praise proper behavior, while Americans only said, "Good." French was a storehouse of beautiful phrases, but I wanted to learn more: I dreamed of one day studying a variety of languages—Japanese, Italian, Russian, German—so that I might find words to express every nuance of emotion and thought.

Although we spoke French at home—my parents pretending it was the only language they understood—I had quickly mastered English on the streets, learning from the grandchildren of the elderly Russian Jewish woman from whom we rented a room after our arrival in the United States. Proud of my new skill, I became my parents' precocious interpreter, helping them negotiate the subtleties of speaking with shopkeepers and officials—always careful to enunciate clearly, with no trace of an accent. (Even today, acquaintances are surprised to learn I grew up in New York; "You have no accent," they say. "I know," I tell them. "I intended not to.") At school, I excelled in English, writing compositions to showcase the arcane vocabulary and complex syntax I had acquired from reading too many nineteenth-century novels too early. In choosing language, I chose the path I thought would lead *away* from home and its ambiguities of identity, unaware that in the end it would guide me even more inexorably back.

◆

When I moved into my first apartment at eighteen, I brought books and clothes. No pots or pans or even recipes. Somehow I managed to avoid learning to cook until I was well into my twenties—and then it was only because I was invited to write a cookbook, a collection of recipes from inexpensive restaurants in New York. Although I protested that I knew nothing about cooking, the men who hired me promised I would learn as I went along. Tempted by the opportunity to be paid for my writing—even if it *was* only a cookbook and not a novel or a dissertation, and even *if* my name would not appear on the title page—for two years I roamed the city, interviewing the owners and cooks in small, ethnic restaurants. The women and men I met were not unlike my mother—recent immigrants to the United States who revived their pasts in the form of care-fully remembered and re-created food. And because many of the people I spoke to knew little English—and because I did not know Greek or Russian or Chinese—food finally became our common language.

With one refugee from Hungary, I spent several afternoons savoring the delicacy of her *paprikash*, simmered with tomatoes and peppers; in a tiny Mexican restaurant on the Upper West Side, I was introduced to *cilantro fino*, a delicate herb with a strong lemon-sharp taste; on the Lower East Side, an elderly Russian Jewish man showed me how to prepare mushroom barley soup, sweetened with sugar and mellowed with warm butter. Often unable to ascertain the names of ingredients in English, I memorized the look and the scent of them, went out into markets with Spanish or Japanese or Russian syllables at the tip of my tongue. In this way, I learned to cook. Not from my mother, but from her surrogates. And not because I cared

31

about cooking, but because I wanted to write. From time to time, while working on the book, I would call to ask my mother's advice: What exactly is a "pinch"? How big is an "average" clove of garlic? In time, I began to ask for *her* recipes, wanting to re-create for myself the *cousa be gebna, m'gaddareh*, and *roz wi loubia wi hamoud* of my childhood. Like the other cooks I met, my mother found it difficult to explain exactly what she did. I had to watch, to taste, to try—practicing patience as I drafted and revised. Over time, I began to acquire my mother's skills; I learned how to feed myself.

◆

A recipe my mother couldn't share, though, was the one for *ful medammes*, the staple food of Egypt. For *ful* was my father's specialty. Only he knew its dark, musky secrets. Throughout my childhood, once a month, on a Sunday morning, he would preside over its ritual preparation. My mother would have gathered the ingredients in advance: canned fava beans imported from Egypt or Lebanon, hard-boiled eggs, cumin, fresh lemon juice, olive oil, *tahina*, and a spicy salad of wilted lettuce and tomatoes. But it was my father who assembled these elements in the distinctive manner that gave the *ful* the texture and flavor I loved.

At exactly 9:00 a.m., he would summon us to join him at the polished mahogany table that dominated our living room. He sat at one end, before a bowl of warmed fava beans, with the eggs, cumin, salt, lemon juice, and olive oil arrayed nearby. Using the tines of a fork, he mashed the beans, working the eggs in one by one. As the dark brown of the beans softened, mellowing with the yellow and white of the eggs, he would begin to add the condiments, mixing and tasting after each addition. My role was that of judge: Were the proportions exactly right? "No," I would say, after taking a taste, "it needs salt." Or, "You need to add lemon juice. More cumin." I was insistent about the cumin—*kamoun*—for more than any one else in the family, I loved its pungent, sharp flavor. If I could choose only one spice to represent for me the rich taste of my childhood, the taste of my parents' remembered Egypt, it would be *kamoun*—fresh, dark, pungent, grainy *kamoun*.

We could purchase the ingredients for *ful medammes*—along with the spices, breads, and other imported delicacies that gave our meals their special character—in only one place: "*Chez les Arabes,*" my mother would say. "At the Arabs," on Atlantic Avenue in downtown Brooklyn. "Ahtlahntique Ahvenue." The name of the street, pronounced with the distinctive French-Arab lilt of my parents' speech, evoked for me dreams of vastness, of ships carrying spices and preserves, of a realm of adventure and enterprise just beyond our horizon. Ahtlahntique Ahvenue. We went there once a month, always on Saturdays, so that my father, whose long working hours usually prevented him from partaking in family activities, might accompany us. We took the car, because it was too long a trip on the subway, and we always came home with multiple bags of groceries to put away.

On Atlantic Avenue, where the plaintive sounds of Arabic music wafted from storefronts and second-story windows, where the men seemed gentler than the women and the children played freely on the sidewalks, my parents relaxed their usual guard, moving easily through the crowd, joking with shopkeepers or talking quietly with one another. Here, more than anywhere in New York, they seemed to belong.

"*Ezayyak?*" the dark-eyed man behind the tall glass case at Sahadi's would ask my father as we entered. "How are you?" And he would nod toward all of us, extending his arm in warm welcome.

"*Quias,*" my father would reply. "Fine." His eyes had a sparkle I seldom saw, and he too would nod his head almost imperceptibly, then hold it up proudly.

"How's business?" he would ask the storekeeper in Arabic.

"Can't complain. *Mabsout,*" the shopkeeper would reply with a shrug. "Good enough."

The two men would go on to genial comments about their health, the weather, their families. The store was inevitably crowded, with customers clamoring for service, but the man at the front always had time for this talk with my father.

"*Itfaddal,*" he would say to us all with a generous sweep of his arm. "Come in." And then he would add that ubiquitous Arabic phrase of hospitality and friendship, "*Ahlan wa sahlan*"— literally, "family" and "plain," but used to mean, "Make yourself at home," or "With us, you are part of the family; may you tread an easy path."

While the men chatted and my mother began the serious business of selecting cheeses and *halawah*, I would drift over to the large barrels of olives pushed against the side wall. There were green, black, greenish-black, big, small, smooth, wrinkled olives—all hidden just below the surface of the dark brine. I wanted to plunge my hands, to submerge my face in the dark sweet water, to let my tongue explore the varied textures and tastes. Beside the olives were bins of grain— bulgur in three different grades (we would buy the fine for tabbouleh, the medium for *kobéba*, the coarse for *burghul* and *kibbe*), along with rice, millet, semolina, couscous. Nearby were dried beans in an assortment of shapes and sizes, a kaleidoscope of muted colors. I loved the red, yellow, and brown of the flat round lentils, the green of the kidney-shaped favas, the gold of the spherical chickpeas. I had to resist running my hands through the bins, feeling the hard beans clicking against one another, letting them fall through my fingers And as if all this dizzying, delicious abundance wasn't enough, there were also the burlap bags filled with spices and herbs—cinnamon, cumin, coriander, dried mint—mingling their scents with that of the dark, finely ground Turkish coffee stored behind the counter.

I hated to leave Sahadi's, knowing we might not return for a month, but my parents always saved the best part of Atlantic Avenue for last, our descent into the bakery, where we would buy the fresh Arabic bread, *pain shami*, we could not do without.

In the 1950s in Brooklyn, the only place one could find Arabic bread was on Atlantic Avenue. These days, packaged pita bread is available in most supermarkets—yet I cannot bring myself to buy it. In New Orleans, I make my way to the Daily Pita Bakery, which supplies the local Arab community.

"What do you call this bread in Arabic?" I ask the soft-spoken Palestinian woman who serves me. "Isn't *pita* the Israeli name for this bread?"

"Yes," she says, "in Arabic it's called *chammedz*."

"*Chammedz*," I repeat after her until I get it right, "*chammedz*. It's strange, isn't it, that Americans call it 'pita,' when it's mostly Arabs, not Israelis, who bake and sell it. You must find that strange."

"Yes," she agrees quietly, "it's strange." The restaurant adjacent to the bakery/grocery store is adorned with a mural of the Dome of the Rock; anti-Israel sentiment is strong here, yet the owners welcome me. They know that I was born in Cairo, and that my family is Jewish. We look directly into each other's eyes when we talk about events in the Middle East and I ask for news of their families on the West Bank. "Where have you been?" the owner asks if I have not come by for a while. "We missed you."

◆

The trip to the bakery on Atlantic Avenue had for my family the aura of pilgrimage. Reached by a narrow flight of concrete stairs leading below the sidewalk to a basement, the bakery was in a low-ceilinged, dark room, with barely space to stand. To the left was a long glass counter, behind which white-shirted men talked briskly in Arabic as they mixed and kneaded the dough. Behind the counter and to the left—I had to lean way over to see it—was the huge brick oven, built into the wall, glowing red, into which flat circles of dough were inserted on long-handled wooden platters. Once in the oven, the loaves ballooned upward, transforming from white disks to pale beige spheres, lightly flecked with brown. Within minutes, they would be slipped out again; on the counter, they slowly deflated. We always bought our bread hot, fresh. It had a fine layer of powdery dry flour on top; inside it was warm and soft, pulling apart into fine sticky webs.

◆

Returning from Atlantic Avenue, smelling the bread and spices in the backseat of the car, I would be deeply satisfied, at peace. For on Atlantic Avenue I had found the accents and aromas and inflections of home, out in the world, beyond the narrow confines of our apartment. On this street no one asked me what kind of person I was, and I had nothing to explain. I saw people who looked like me and ate like me, dark-skinned children and adults with eyes like mine. Here my parents lapsed into the rhythms and gestures of their own childhoods, and I too could let myself go. It seemed clear on Atlantic Avenue that I was Middle Eastern, Egyptian. For a moment, I knew who I was.

Yet even then my confidence was flawed; a gap prevented my complete identification. It was not simply that I retained an awareness of being Jewish, conscious that the Arabs were—what?—"*Musulman*," I had been told. "Muslim." Much more significant was the fact that I could not speak the language of these people I so obviously resembled and with whom I felt such an affinity. I could utter not a word of Arabic. So when my father spoke to the store owner, I didn't really know what they said. When the man helping my mother asked her a question—perhaps it was about me—I could make no sense of her reply. I was, indeed, at home on Atlantic Avenue, but it was the pre-linguistic at-homeness of someone who can neither understand nor make herself understood.

Although they spoke it occasionally between themselves, my parents never taught me to speak Arabic. I heard greetings, prayers, invocations, thanks: *salaamtek, in sha'allah, hamdulillah, mabrouk*. The word used most often by relatives to describe me, *aroosa*—bride—was Arabic. "*In sha'allah aroosa*," they always said. "God willing that you will be a bride." But my parents didn't think it necessary for me to learn the language they reserved for expressing their strongest feelings. What occasion would I have for it, they wondered, when I told them I wanted to learn it. The obvious answer, to speak with other Egyptians, did not arise.

"If you're from Egypt, then how come you don't speak Egyptian?" acquaintances still ask, and I struggle to explain the racism and elitism that shame me.

"The middle-class Jews in Egypt," I say, "wanted to distinguish themselves from the Arabs; they wanted to stay separate. So, if they could afford it, they sent their children to French schools. The French had set up schools in Egypt in the nineteenth century, after Napoleon invaded the country. French became the preferred language of the middle-class Jews, allowing them to think of themselves as European rather than Arab. And besides, there is no such thing as 'Egyptian.' The language Egyptians speak is Arabic."

"You mean you don't speak Yiddish?"

I'm back in the schoolyard again. How can I explain?

"No, we spoke French at home," I repeat, irritated, embarrassed. "We didn't speak Yiddish." Yiddish was another one of those markers of true Jewishness our family failed to possess. But speaking Yiddish is beside the point. It's Arabic I don't speak, Arabic I need to learn.

◆

My father spoke perfect Egyptian Arabic, having worked for nearly twenty years as an interpreter in the Mixed Courts in Cairo. In New York, while I was growing up, he occasionally contracted to do small translation jobs, bringing his assignments home, spreading papers and dictionaries around him in the living room. He admired and appreciated the language, boasting to me of its flexibility, its poetic resources. To indicate that a woman is beautiful, for example, you can say, "The distance between the bottom of her earrings and the top of her shoulders is very great."

My mother is less fluent, cannot read or write Arabic, her formal education having been in French and British English. She mastered French, though her English remained halting, even after she came to the United States. For a few years a teacher in her lycée made an effort to teach the girls Arabic; whenever they came to a certain passage, early in the grammar book—my mother remembers the words in French, *"Ahmadou grimpé sur le palmier,"* which means, "Ahmed climbs on the palm tree"— they gave up and went back to the beginning. When I ask her why she didn't try to study on her own, she says that Arabic is an ugly language, like German, with its harsh gutturals. She tells me that *les Arabes*, those generous people we saw on Atlantic Avenue each month, are not like us. They are not *comme il faut*— proper. *"Ils ne sont pas eduqués,"* she says, as if this will clinch it. "They are uneducated." Indeed, my mother continues, Arabs live like animals; they are dirty, dangerous, dark. In the 1940s they had threatened the Jews in Cairo; today, they menace the state of Israel. Why would I want to speak their language?

I strive to understand my mother's perspective, to make allowances for her experience. Growing up, she had few opportunities to interact with non-Jewish Egyptians other than servants or merchants, and these people she had been taught to keep at a distance. Dark skinned, dark eyed, and dark haired herself, she might easily have passed as the native she was: Her father regularly upbraided her for being too dark, calling her *un poux dans du lait*, a louse in milk.

I recall our trip to Brazil when I was eight years old, to visit my maternal relatives who had immigrated there in 1956. After a week at the beach with my mother and her sister, we returned to São Paulo, where my grandfather pointed at my knees and told me they needed scrubbing. I went to the bathroom and washed them roughly with a stiff cloth. When I returned he told me I was still dirty. I washed again. The third time I came into the living room, he pointed at my knees and raised his voice in anger: I looked like *une Arabe*, he shouted, my mother shouldn't have allowed me to stay in the sun. Confused and ashamed, I wondered what I had done. What was it to be *une Arabe*, and why was it so bad? If these people were so different from us—and somehow worse—why did we eat the same food? Why did my parents speak their language? How could a whole people be bad? My mother told me to be silent, to behave myself. She knew about these things, she said, and maybe when I got older I would understand.

But of course as I have gotten older, I have understood less and less. I am over fifty, with a Ph.D. in literature and a good job at a university. I have studied French, German, Latin, Greek. When I traveled as a child with my family to South America, I found myself easily acquiring bits of Spanish and Portuguese. In Italy a few years ago, I spoke comfortably with taxi drivers and waiters; in Hungary, I survived on an amalgam of French and German. I am never so happy as when I am learning a new language. Yet I have never applied myself to the study of Arabic. Once, in my early twenties, I persuaded my father to teach me. After a few evenings struggling to shape the letters, I gave up. The distance was too great, the syntax too foreign—and I could sense my mother's disapproval.

Because I have never learned the language of my homeland, there has been a strange lacuna in my identity, a wound I have been unable to heal. I cook Arabic food and shop in Arab markets, but I cannot, must not, it seems, speak the words of the people who also eat that food and shop in those markets. The Jewish part of my identity is by now relatively unproblematic. Whether or not I grew up eating gefilte fish or keeping kosher, I know that I am, by birth and custom and some fragments of belief, Jewish. But the Egyptian part remains unfulfilled, incomplete. To claim it, I must do more than stuff grape leaves and buy fresh Arabic bread. I must learn the language of my homeland.

◆

Living away from the East Coast of the United States for twenty years, I have been lonely for my kind. But who are my kind? When I meet Jewish women from New York, we instantly gravitate toward one another. We appreciate each other's jokes, understand references, share a rhythm and a style. For a brief moment, I can feel that I am not too loud, that I am not at all pushy, that I can let my intelligence and wit have free rein. I am at home. And I think, yes, that's who I am, I'm a Jew from New York.

But recently I found myself in different company. I had arranged a meeting with a new friend, an Egyptian Muslim who teaches in Washington, D.C. Mervat had brought along another woman, an Egyptian who teaches at Cairo University. We were together to explore what it might mean to imagine a community of contemporary Egyptian women that includes both Muslims and Jews. We had tea at my brother's Georgetown house, then met a few days later for coffee at Union Station. (I had offered to cook a meal—I was thinking of *hamoud* and *loubia*, perhaps some *ba'alawa* or *fila au fromage*—but Mervat said briskly, "No, you're on vacation, you don't need to be slaving away in the kitchen! I'll bring pastries and you prepare the tea.")

Sitting with Mervat and Hoda, women who look more like me than anyone I have met before, I find myself relaxing in a new way, the way I think my father must have relaxed all those years ago at Sahadi's. We speak to each other with our eyes, our hands, the play of a muscle above an eyebrow. Our words in English barely skim the surface; something else is going on. When Hoda and Mervat confer with each other rapidly in Arabic I listen hungrily, hovering on the brink of understanding. At one point, Hoda insists on paying for my coffee. At first I protest, then I acquiesce. She has made a slight gesture with her hand, indicating it would be discourteous of me to deny her this pleasure. I understand the gesture and the lifting of her eyebrows. An Arabic gesture. An Egyptian impulse of hospitality. What would happen between us, I wonder, if we could speak together in Arabic, entirely bypassing the European tongue?

I notice my handwriting now as I hurry to capture these thoughts. It is a highly stylized, sweeping script. I see with new eyes its elaborate flourishes and loops, the dots over my i's that could be dashes, the stops and starts as letters are connected or not. Although I write with a lead pencil, there is subtle shading as well, with some lines thicker or thinner, as if I were using a calligraphic pen. If I squint, if I view it from a certain angle, I can see my writing moving toward another ideal, a different alphabet. *Alif. Ba.* The names of the letters in Arabic. I make the commitment. I will study Arabic.

At the university where I teach, I sign up for a course in the evening division. My instructor is a young graduate student from Jordan; he has the bright black eyes and dark skin that remind me of the men in my family; he could be my brother, my cousin. Twice a week, I repeat with him the sounds I have heard since childhood, only now they are accompanied by grammar and spelling, imbued with meaning. Painstakingly, I learn the alphabet, practice reading from right to left. At night, I listen to tapes before going to sleep, I write out vocabulary on small cards and test myself. I learn the numbers from 1 to 10; the days of the week; standard greetings; the words for man, woman, child. But my other obligations press. There are papers to grade and lectures to prepare. After a year, I have made little progress, but I remain fitfully committed. At the very least, I console myself, when I finally go to Cairo I will be able to read a street sign; I will know how to order tea, *bel ne'na'*, with mint. In the market, I will know how to find *kamoun*. I will know the Arabic words for grape leaves. And the next time I am invited to a potluck party in the United States, I will again make the dish I love so much. Only this time I will be chatting in Arabic with new friends; we will move in concert as we bend to the rhythms of peeling, mincing, stuffing, rolling. Each leaf will fall easily into place, for I will at last be able to nourish myself with words, aromatic words that fill my mouth with their rich consonants and moist vowels, words that fill my belly with the sweet, rich juice of communion.

Three: Rose

◆ ◆ ◆

It wasn't until I was twenty-five and studying belly dance that I learned to listen to Middle Eastern music. I had ventured into the class on a whim, inspired by a friend who idolized her teacher, a sixty-five-year-old American woman married to a

Rose Zonana with Nelly and Felix on their honeymoon, Palestine, 1945.

Moroccan man. Violet was slender, too thin for a belly dancer really, with long black hair and strong blue eyes that gazed directly out from a carefully made-up face. She wore plain black leotards accented by a silk scarf tied loosely around her hips; her toenails and fingernails were lacquered bright red. Her bare studio, perched on a steep San Francisco hill, occupied the lower level of her house. A pristine, inviolate space with a floor-to-ceiling mirror covering a long wall, it opened onto a garden, richly green.

In that room, in a world apart, Violet taught us—her willing acolytes—to arch our backs, to circle our bellies and breasts, to roll our shoulders and rotate our hips in slow arcs. She encouraged us to close our eyes and to bend our knees, to open our arms and to let the music rise from the soles of our feet to the crowns of our heads. Working deliberately, she led us in delicate hand gestures and intricate footsteps, demonstrating how our bodies might register each quaver, each beat of the pulsing, sinuous sound. She taught us to play finger cymbals, to drape scarves across our heads and arms, to tie them around our hips. And then, stretched along the floor, she showed us how to unveil, carefully revealing ourselves.

Violet's classes met for two hours, three times a week. Our sessions began with leisurely stretches and methodical foot massage—each of us seated on an antique prayer rug—and ended in wild shimmies, the rugs pushed aside, our cymbals ringing, the studio a whirl of ecstatic movement and sound. Often during the last half hour her husband, Mahsoud, would join us, tapping out a beat on his North African drums.

Leaving San Francisco meant leaving Violet. And although I never found her equal, I have studied belly dance off and on ever since—in Philadelphia, Oklahoma, and New Orleans—seeking teachers with a similar veneration for this ancient form. Rock and roll, country and western, blues, jazz, the zydeco and Cajun sounds of Louisiana—all of these delight me. But it is only Middle Eastern music that I find irresistible, that rouses me from whatever torpor has benumbed me, pulling me inexorably onto my feet. Hearing its familiar sounds, I close my eyes, I lift my arms, I bend my knees, and my hips begin to trace slow circles; my hair—whatever its actual length—brushes my shoulders; my earrings and bracelets jingle; I stretch into my belly and breasts. The evocative call of the flute, the plaintive sounds of the oud call me back into my Self, and I move with the rhythm of my blood.

◆

Before my discovery of belly dance at twenty-five, I perceived Arabic music only with my mother's ears, hearing nothing but a cacophony of empty sound.

"I hate it," my mother would say. "It's ugly and sad."

If my mother could have had her way, our Brooklyn apartment would have been filled only with the studiously upbeat sound of 1950s popular music, supplemented by Italian opera, *Live From the Met* on Saturday afternoons. But my mother's authority was limited; she was subject, even in the home she managed so well, to the will of her mother-in-law, my father's widowed mother, *Nonna*—the woman who, with the exception of the five years between my parents' emigration from Cairo and hers, lived with my parents from the day of their wedding in 1945 until the day they placed her in a nursing home, in 1975.

I will never know which came first: my mother's distaste for Middle Eastern music or her conflict with her mother-in-law. I only know that in the unspoken battleground that was our home, my grandmother's music came to represent all that my mother abhorred. Given the choices—my vibrant mother or my embittered grandmother—I aligned myself with my mother, barricading myself against the sounds of my birthplace, refusing to hear my grandmother's call.

For *Nonna* cherished Arabic music, listening to it daily despite my mother's obvious distaste. She would sit alone in the center of the worn sofa bed that stretched along one wall of our living room, an embroidered and perfumed handkerchief in her hand, her records beside her. She had only four—scratched recordings of popular favorites by Fairuz, the Lebanese diva, and Farid Al-Atrash, an Egyptian heartthrob—yet she played them, one after another, day after day, year after year, on the old Victrola in the corner. Hearing the plaintive, mournful sounds, I could not distinguish the seemingly endless repetition of the songs themselves from the repetition caused by the needle skipping across the battered old disks. The Arabic words were incomprehensible to me, the music discordant and strange; yet for *Nonna*, locked in her memories, these were the sounds of home.

As she listened, repeating the Arabic words and humming the tunes, she would begin to rock, sighing, crying, working herself into a paroxysm of pain. "Aiii," she keened as Fairuz's voice rose in an anthem of love for her lost Lebanon, "aiii." Instead of mourning Lebanon, *Nonna* lamented her sons Ezra and Isaac, my father's two brothers, who lived abroad; she mourned for a daughter who died in infancy, for a husband dead after only ten years of marriage. "Aiiiii," *Nonna* cried, the sound now rising from her chest, simultaneously deep and shrill. All that had been left behind—her country, her family, her youth, her joy—contributed to this fathomless, endless, encompassing, grief. And that grief wound itself so fully into the music that those songs, whatever their lyrics or rhythm—whether folk ballad or love song or playful melody—came to represent for me an echoing litany of loss.

Terrified and threatened by the immensity of her grief, the fixity of her pain, I wanted my aging *Nonna* gone, away from our home, out of our lives, so that I might give myself to the unthinking pleasures of my own young body. If I could have, I would have stopped my ears against the sound, run into my room, locked the door, and never emerged. But the only room I had was the one I shared with *Nonna*, and, trained as I was to be a good girl—*une fille bien élevée*—all I could do was avert my eyes from the sight of her huddled on the sofa. For many years, the sound of Arabic music elicited in me an immediate, visceral response: My stomach clenched and I grew rigid with distress. *Nonna* came back to me, in all her suffering. So when I stepped into that dance studio in San Francisco, I was already moving with a new freedom: I was beginning to reoccupy the body *Nonna* had so savagely possessed.

◆

Rose Zonana, my father's mother, immigrated to the United States in 1956 and lived with our family in Brooklyn for nearly twenty years. Born Rose Beyda in Aleppo in 1887, she had grown to young womanhood in a large, prosperous family of Jewish merchants. She had five brothers—David, Daniel, Clement, Ezra, and Gabriel—and two sisters, Jeanne and Sarah. When I knew her, only her brothers David and Daniel were still alive. Although she was not close to either of them, her nieces and nephews, my father's cousins—Sheila, Henri, Joseph, Gabriel, Lisette, Leah, Shelley, Alfred, Edmond, and Esther—hovered at the edges of our lives, visiting at holidays, offering homage to *Nonna*—*la Tante* Rose, they called her, the Aunt Rose—regaling her with stories of engagements and weddings, births and bar mitzvahs. The children of these cousins—Colette, André, Vivianne, David, Billy, Amy, Daniel, Janine, Joan, May, Steve, Cynthia, Irving—were *my* peers, the relatives among whom it was expected I would find my intimate friends, my own future spouse. For in the Beyda family, cousins married cousins, uncles married nieces, pairs of brothers married pairs of sisters: The family was a vine, not a tree, a tangle of interwoven relations.

And *Nonna* was mistress of those relations, with a keen memory for the intricacies of bloodlines and alliances; she knew the secrets of all these mothers and fathers and children, cousins and cousins of cousins, and she took pleasure in remembering and recounting all the degrees, not of separation, but of closeness. She herself had married at twenty-two, in 1909, accepting the offer of a wool merchant ten years her senior—someone *not* in the extended family, and not considered an especially good prospect by the well-to-do Beyda clan. Still, he persuaded her father, and Rose married. It must have been a love match. His name was Vita Zonana, the only son of a Talmudic scholar, Itzhak—himself an only son—reputed to have died in a fire. "They say his lamp overturned while he was studying," my father told me of his paternal grandfather, my great grandfather, a man he never met. I visualize red flames rising from a tattered Hebrew text. Itzhak would have been alone, studying at night in an otherwise darkened room, on the silent second floor of an ancient house. I see old Turkish rugs, heavy drapes, papers scattered on the small wooden desk. The fire would build rapidly, engulfing Itzhak before he could cry out. But the words of God were on his lips, the mystic letters before his eyes. I imagine Itzhak's end: consumed by the flame of devotion, held in the burning eye of God. I welcome him as an ancestor, this man who left no trace but this fragment of a story, not even a story really, but a vision, a dream of holy fire.

I know equally little about Itzhak's son, my grandfather Vita, *Nonna*'s husband—although he too is distinguished largely by his death—an early death in 1919, at forty-two, after only ten years of marriage. "I was an orphan, you know," my father explained, offering a clue to his own melancholy, his own sense of displacement. There are no photographs, no mementos of the absent Vita—only one story, told to me by my mother in hushed secrecy: "Your grandfather died of typhoid; he was on a trip to Upper Egypt, selling fabric; he got very sick and died in three days." Rose was by then thirty-two, a mother of three boys, living in the Cairo suburb of Heliopolis. Convinced that her husband's death was caused by his contact with poor village Arabs, she swore that her children would become educated professionals, with jobs in the European center of Cairo. She became obsessed with the threat of infection, terrified by the prospect of disease, afraid of the dangers that might lie in wait outside her home. She became a recluse, rarely leaving the house; all animals were anathema, dirt was vigorously attacked, and touch—of any kind—was discouraged.

I remember tickling my brother when he was an infant. "Don't touch the baby!" *Nonna* cried, "You'll make him sick." (Was she thinking of her own little girl—whose name was never spoken—who had died before turning two?)

At night, in bed, I would enjoy doing exercises, arching my back, raising my buttocks, and circling my legs in an inverted bicycle.

"Don't move," *Nonna* would say. "You'll hurt yourself." And later, "Don't go down the street. Don't go into the city. Don't. Don't. Don't." (Was she thinking of her husband, dead because he traveled from Cairo?)

When I begged to have a pet, a dog or a cat that I might cuddle and hold, my grandmother was horrified. I was eventually allowed to buy several goldfish, but when they jumped from their small tank onto our bedroom floor, it was out of the question to get new ones. My brother briefly kept a chameleon, and once, we had a turtle. Both escaped their cages and were found beneath her bed. She accused us of trying to kill her. *"Tu veux me tuer!"*

◆

Nonna never remarried after her husband's death, choosing instead to live with her mother and mother-in-law. Before they were fourteen, her eldest sons—my father, Felix, and his older brother, Isaac—were working to earn money for the family. Rose left the management of the household to her mother and mother-in-law while she spent her afternoons playing cards. When Isaac grew old enough to marry, he chose a Beyda cousin and moved to Zagazig, a city several hours north in the Nile Delta. Ezra, her youngest son, became a leader of Cairo's Zionist youth movement and left for Palestine in the early 1940s, helping to found a kibbutz and fighting for the establishment of the state of Israel. Only Felix, the middle son, remained with Rose at home. And when he married in 1945, he brought his wife—my mother—to live in the apartment in which he had grown up.

◆

"I blame your mother's mother," *Tante* Suze tells me, as we talk about the early days of my parents' marriage. "She should have encouraged your mother to stand up for herself. Instead, she told her to submit. She told her she had to accept."

For Rose did not take kindly to the young woman my father brought into her home. Even before the wedding, she made her jealousy plain, demanding a trousseau of silk nightgowns and embroidered undergarments to match the ones being prepared for the young bride. She accompanied the newlyweds on their honeymoon in Palestine, and when they returned to Cairo, she collapsed, crying every night on the floor outside my parents' bedroom, sobbing until my father came out to console her. She missed her other sons, she said. She had been abandoned; no one cared for her. When my parents wanted to go out for the evening, *Nonna* threatened to die while they were out. "*Je vais mourir!*" she shrieked.

Today *Nonna* would, one hopes, be diagnosed as the deeply disturbed woman that she was and given medication or therapy to assuage her. My mother would be encouraged to leave her husband if nothing changed, and my father would be urged to pay more attention to his wife than to his mother. But in Cairo in the 1940s submission to a mother-in-law was taken for granted. That this mother-in-law's demands exceeded the bounds of reason was immaterial. The family shaped itself to accommodate—and incorporate—her pain.

◆

When my parents departed Egypt in 1951, they left *Nonna* behind with her eldest son, Isaac, and his family, saying they would be away for no more than two weeks. My cousins recall the day she was told that Felix and Nelly and the baby were not coming back. "*C'était térrible,*" they tell me. "It was terrible. You could hear her screams throughout the entire apartment building." But for my mother, what a lovely reprieve! During our first few years in the United States, we lived in a rented room in a Russian Jewish family's Brooklyn home; my father worked long hours at poorly paying jobs and underwent several surgeries; my mother was forced to spend nine months in bed while pregnant with my brother. Still, these hardships must have seemed easy in comparison to life with *Nonna.* But in 1956, my mother's brief idyll was over. The Suez War prompted most Jews to flee Egypt. My father managed to obtain an entrance visa for *Nonna.* Soon she would be joining us.

◆

As we did for all relatives arriving from abroad, we went to the airport en masse to greet *Nonna*'s flight from London. This time, though, our usual anticipation was dulled by dread. I know that at seven I didn't consciously remember the elderly woman I had lived with as an infant in Cairo, but her personality must have left its imprint on my psyche. Certainly I could sense my mother's anxiety as I stood at her side, holding her cold, inert hand. I wanted to ask questions, but I knew I would receive empty answers. I had been told to be a good girl, to demonstrate that I was *bien élevée.* I was to love *Nonna* and respect her; she was old and I was young. It was the duty of the young to respect the old. From now on, my mother told me, *Nonna* and I would be sharing a room.

The meeting with *Nonna* at the airport figures for me as a stark drama on a bare set: I see no one there but myself, my mother, and an old woman dimly framed in a long, empty corridor. Surely there were others—arriving passengers, their relatives and friends, my own father and young brother. But in memory I retain only an image of a grim encounter between three females of three generations. What do we say? What do we do? Are there tears, exclamations? Do we touch? Kiss? On one cheek or two? My memory fails, except to suggest the progressive stiffening, the rigid fear that overcame me. It is as if I lose all consciousness, become motionless, voiceless, sightless, deaf. I see myself dropping away, falling, lost.

But no, this can't be right. No one else remembers such a moment. I must be confusing *Nonna*'s arrival with something else, something that happened years later, something I never experienced but have been told. The year is 1968, not 1956, and I am nineteen, not seven. I have just moved away from home; at the same time, *Nonna* has been in Europe, visiting Isaac. My parents have gone to the airport to meet her, and, as she emerges from customs, she asks about me. They tell her that I have moved out, that I am living in my own apartment. The news stuns her—it is *honteux*, she cries, shameful, for an unmarried girl to live alone, what will people think? Within moments, she faints, falling to the airport floor. The emergency medical team is summoned, and she is taken by ambulance to a hospital.

So it is my grandmother, not I, who faints, and it is because of my absence, not her presence. But in the confusion of identities that is our family, I cannot make distinctions. Someone fainted at an airport; someone was overwhelmed by someone else. My grandmother's arrival, my own departure: They are one.

◆

The woman I encountered that day in 1956 seemed old, older than anyone I had known before—though I see now that *Nonna* was not yet seventy, not much older than Violet when I studied dance with her in San Francisco. But *Nonna* at seventy had long since abandoned her body. Whatever pleasures she may have known as a young woman, she had long since come to regard her physical existence as a burden, an encumbrance. Even as a child I recognized her deep withdrawal from the senses, and I feared that she might pull me into the same cold hardness. Her dull gray hair was arranged in tight ridges, crinkled waves that reflected and amplified the deep wrinkles of her face. Her eyes were set far back, beneath a wide forehead and beside a long, sharp nose. One eye winked shut while the other stared forward. The mass of her body was indistinct, shapeless, as if she could no longer summon the will to remain erect. A knitted wool skirt, with an uneven hem, hung gracelessly, falling just above her thick, stocking-clad ankles. She appeared lopsided, wavering, off balance.

Later, I learned that *Nonna* had been diagnosed with breast cancer a few years before coming to the United States. The mastectomy left her palpably wounded, and though she tried to conceal her torso's lack of symmetry by draping scarves across her shoulder, she always appeared to be visibly maimed. And every night for seven years, in the privacy of the room we shared, I was witness to the extent of her scar. Although she tried to turn away from me, each night I watched as she slowly removed her skirt, blouse, and bra. Inside the bra was a flesh-colored foam pad she would carefully fold and place in a drawer. I perceived that there was a gap where her breast should be, but I never understood—or asked—why this might be so.

Nonna's deformed and aging body, so close to my young one in that narrow bedroom, grew more than monstrous in my imagination. Her flesh was pale, cold, spotted; in addition to the missing breast, there were false teeth. These too she removed nightly, placing them in a battered tin cup on a small table at her bedside. The dentures clattered against the old metal, glistening eerily beneath the surface of the water. Without her teeth, *Nonna's* lips folded inward, losing shape; her mouth became a vacant hole from which her words fell loosely. I was the only one who heard these words she spoke in the night—words in French and Arabic, words of sorrow and despair, words that found their way into my dreams, leaving me as desolate and lonely as she.

Sharing a room with *Nonna*, I was convinced that one of the illustrated fairy tales in my Golden Books had come to life. *Nonna* was my own wicked stepmother, a witch intent on harming me. I thought of the wolf that had swallowed Little Red

Riding Hood's grandmother. Could *Nonna* be such a predator? In the top drawer of her dresser, *Nonna* kept a small tin filled with hard candies. "Take one," she would offer, but I refused, fearing what might happen if I ate, remembering Hansel and Gretel, fearing that I might be swallowed whole myself.

But although I never ate the sweets *Nonna* offered, I could not fully inure myself to her presence. Lying beside her, my own body became strange and unfamiliar, swollen and distended. Like her, I grew awkward and ungainly, my impulse toward movement thwarted and restrained. Unable physically to escape our enforced intimacy, I learned to slip away secretly in my mind—to dissociate myself from my actual surroundings, to dwell in a disembodied realm of fantasy and dream. By the age of ten, I had convinced myself that the only reality was the world of ideas; a Platonist long before reading the *Republic*, I distrusted the flesh and believed that only in the mind could one find fulfillment.

◆

I know little of *Nonna*'s real story, nothing about her life as she experienced it. She died when I was twenty-seven; even then, I resisted contact, afraid of what might happen if I got too close. Half-heartedly, I tried to talk with her some months before her death, but our words fell into the empty space between us. After her death, my father mourned for two decades; to this day, my mother is reluctant to talk about her.

When I ask her about those last years with *Nonna* she begins to cry, says, "That's over now. It's in the past, why talk about it?" But I am of that self-willed American generation that believes talking can only heal, not harm. I want to probe, to uncover, to bring to light the secrets we have kept all these years. My mother knows better.

"Will talking change anything?" she asks.

"No," I have to admit.

"Then why talk? There's no use in talking."

◆

During the final years, my mother became *Nonna*'s servant and nurse, bathing her, feeding her, carrying her up and down the stairs of the small house the family had moved to. As she grew older, *Nonna*'s grief grew violent; she became abusive, more overtly paranoid and hostile. Imagining unseen attackers, she accused my mother of plotting to kill her. Unnerved at last, my mother fled to Brazil, to be with her own mother. In her absence, my brother and I held tense meetings with our father, calling on cousins and other relatives for help. *Nonna* would have to go to a nursing home, we insisted. In the end, Felix was persuaded. My mother returned, and *Nonna*—despite her shrieks—was moved to the Sephardic Home for the Aged in Brooklyn. There, for two years, she found a kind of peace—a gallant suitor who brought flowers and candy, old friends from Cairo who spoke to her in Arabic and invited her to join them at cards. My mother visited every day; on the one day she failed to come, my grandmother died.

◆

I try to envision the love my grandmother experienced as a young woman. Did she ever feel passion? Did she know desire? Delight? Joy? As an old woman, she could still be coquettish. Although her body was tired and her clothes unfashionable, she enjoyed dressing up. "*Elle aime se farder*," my mother would say, with a hint of contempt. "She likes to make up." *Nonna* kept a drawerful of scarves, bracelets, large enameled earrings that she took out for special occasions. When relatives complimented her, she blushed, became playful, even flirtatious. "She used to be the life of the party," one of my cousins told me. "As a girl she had many admirers."

Yet for fifty-five years, as far as I can calculate, my grandmother lived without sexual touch—from the time of her husband's death when she was thirty-two until her own death at eighty-seven. I try to imagine such a life, to enter the body of a woman who has borne four children and will never again know the sensations of limbs twined, bellies pressed together. Why did she never remarry? "It wasn't done," my relatives tell me. "She was dedicated to her sons." But once the sons were grown? What was it like for her to live with my father and his wife, to sense their love? How did she feel when I became a restless adolescent? When I began to kiss and be fondled by the boys who walked me home from school?

◆

My dance teacher in New Orleans was a young woman, not yet thirty-five. With soft hips and full breasts, Audrey incarnated the sensuality of the belly dancer. Yet for Audrey—as for Violet—this dance was also deeply spiritual, a ritual offering to the divine. For the true belly dancer, body and spirit are one. Audrey taught several mornings a week, and I went often. Because she didn't have enough space in her small apartment, and because she couldn't afford to rent a studio, she held her classes wherever she could. I'd been with her in the bare exercise room of a fashionable day spa; in the plant-filled loft of a local artist; in the serene, carpeted prayer room of a Krishna devotee. For several months, her classes were held in an apartment I had rented during a separation from Kay.

At 10:00 a.m. on Mondays, Wednesdays, and Fridays, we would gather in my large, sparsely-furnished second-story space. It was early spring in New Orleans, and I would open all the windows, allowing the breeze to blow from the front balcony to the back kitchen. Downstairs, I would leave the front door unlocked for latecomers. After warm-up stretches, we would array ourselves in loose cotton skirts, draping scarves around our hips. Veils of red, blue, and green would drift over us. Her eyes closed, Audrey would lead us as we surrendered to the music.

Afterward, exhausted, we lay beside one another on the

floor. Some mornings Audrey read verses from Rumi; on others, we told our own stories. When the women left, I would lock the downstairs door, find my old recording of Fairuz, and turn up the volume. As I moved through the house, dancing alone, my thoughts would turn to *Nonna*, who remained in my mind, huddled on the old sofa, crying to these very songs.

I have come to love the sounds my grandmother cherished, but for me they are a portal into joyous movement, not a soundtrack of immobile grief. For the most part, the aged *Nonna* I knew no longer stands between me and that music, severing my body from my soul. With each step, with each swirl, I enter more fully into the world she would have known before all her losses, a world in which she loved and was loved, as a young woman, bold and free. Yet often enough, despite what we both might want, she still stops me with her cries.

Four: Allegra ♦ ♦ ♦

I had another *Nonna*, the *Nonna* in Brazil, my mother's mother, Allegra Chalom. As an infant, I was with her often, but after our family left Cairo, I saw her only rarely. She came twice to the United States—once, in 1954 when my brother was born, and again, in 1956, when she stopped briefly in New York while en route to Brazil. Later, my mother took us to South America for two long visits, in 1958 and 1962.

Allegra Chalom, in Cairo, early 1950s.

Although I never really knew her, I loved my *Nonna* in Brazil. And I believed that she loved me. I imagined her to resemble the kindly *bubbas* of our Eastern European Jewish neighbors in Brooklyn; I thought she might be like my best friend Debbie's grandmother, Mrs. Fishkin. Debbie's *bubba*, a well-dressed woman with frosted hair, lived in an immaculate apartment on Eastern Parkway, where she cooked chicken soup every Friday and took Debbie's part in arguments with her mother. Or perhaps *Nonna* was like Mrs. Rosenblum, the elderly Russian matron from whom we had rented a room during our first years in New York. Plump, bustling, self-sufficient, Mrs. Rosenblum sold newspapers at a stand in Manhattan—she was the first working woman I knew. Every morning she rose before dawn and took the subway into the city, coming home in the early afternoon to the three-story frame house she shared with her daughters and grandchildren—and us. Our room was on the first floor, at the back; most days, after she came home, Mrs. Rosenblum would invite me to join her in the kitchen, and I would clamber onto her lap, comforted by her soft warmth. *Nonna* in Brazil must be like Mrs. Rosenblum, I told myself later, a good grandmother to offset the bad one I had at home.

It pained my mother to be separated from this *Nonna*, and, as always, I felt with, or through, my mother. My mother and I look alike; when I was a child, distant relatives coming upon me at a wedding or bar mitzvah always knew: "*Ça doit être la fille de Nelly*," they would say. "You must be Nelly's daughter." Recently, at a gathering in New York of Jews from Egypt, a cousin of my mother's recognized me in an instant: "Nelly," she called across a room, then corrected herself. "No, no, you must be Joyce. Nelly's daughter."

As a child, I reveled in my similarity to my mother. Secretly, I studied her feet and face and hair, enumerating to myself each trait we had in common: the short, gnarled toes; the long, ridged nose; the extravagantly waved black hair. As I grew older and sought a separate identity, our resemblance impeded my quest.

I worked to obscure the obvious, letting my hair grow long, hiding my hips, even dreaming of a nose job. In public, I pretended to be someone else, not at all my mother's daughter. But in my earliest years, it was gratifying to find myself reflected, the solidity of my mother's body helping to assure me of the reality of my own.

From the old photographs, I could see that my mother looked like her mother. Which meant that I looked like *Nonna* too. We were a triptych, Allegra and Nelly and I, united by blood and bone and skin, mirroring one other across continents, through time. No one else in the family looked as we did: We were the vital core, the strong trunk of the family tree. Although as a girl I rarely dreamed of growing up to have a child of my own, when I looked at these photographs I *did* vaguely think about the possibility of having a daughter who might be yet another incarnation of *Nonna*. I pictured to myself an unending sequence of women and girls, mothers and daughters and grandmothers and granddaughters, faces and bodies and eyes reflecting back into the past and forward into the future. And no matter how far the series extended, no matter how many faces reflected one another, always, at the center, would be *Nonna*, our shining original— *Nonna*, my fabulous *Nonna* in Brazil, the wonderful woman whose name I bore.

For in calling me Joyce, my parents had sought an English name that would approximate "Allegra," Italian for "light," "cheerful," "bright." Because they were already planning to immigrate to the United States, they wanted me to have a name that would allow me to fit in. How could they know that no name could give me the ease I desired? That I would covet the lyrical lilt and obscurity of "Allegra," the echoing vowels and rolling *l*'s and *r*, the exotic allure of a name I knew had something to do with music? "Allegra," I would say to myself, "my true name is Allegra, the name of my true *Nonna*."

So it was with eager anticipation that, at the age of eight, I learned that my mother, my brother, and I would be flying to

South America to visit *Nonna* and *Nonno* and the other members of my mother's family who had found their way to Brazil and Colombia. In Cairo, the Chaloms had been a close, warm, bustling family—with several generations and numerous cousins living under one roof. "The table was never set for less than twelve," my mother remembers. But in the United States, we lived as an isolated nuclear family (with the exception of my other *Nonna*), and my mother, unlike my father, had none of her close relatives nearby.

It was March 1958, and I was in the fourth grade. Although we had planned our trip to last a month, we ended up staying for three. Miss Greenberg, my public school teacher, sent me off with homework—a math text and a reader with stories about the Seven Wonders of the World. I remember the Colossus at Rhodes, the Hanging Gardens of Babylon, the Great Pyramids at Giza. I completed all the math exercises and read all the stories on the sixteen-hour flight to Bogotá. So for the next three months, I had no assignments. Released from the structure of school, I was free to fully absorb the strange landscapes and unaccustomed rhythms of life on another continent.

My memories of those months in Colombia and Brazil are thick with sensory detail, rich with the colors and flavors and smells of a different world. Even now I can see the bright green frog we surprised on the grass at the Panama City airport; I taste the sweet juice of the fresh pineapple my aunt bought for me on a busy São Paulo street; I hear the sudden rain splattering the hard soil in Bogotá. Without books, I learned to look and to listen; after a few weeks in Bogotá, I could understand and speak rudimentary Spanish: "*gracias,*" "*por favor,*" "*yo quiero un poquito mas.*" Later, in Brazil, I succumbed to the spell of Portuguese, rolling the strange new vowels and soft consonants around my tongue. Where Spanish had an *n*, Portuguese often used an *m*: "*Um poco,*" I learned to say, and "*Um minuto*"; *l* became *r*, and *aaoouun* was a new sound altogether: "*Saaoouun Paaoouulo,*" I repeated with delight, "*Saaoouun Paaoouulo.*"

Our first stop was Bogotá, where my mother's sister Céline lived in a large house on the outskirts of the city. Céline had left Cairo with her husband and three children the year before we did, in 1950; now, in the spring of 1958, there were seven children—four boys and three girls. The oldest was eighteen, the youngest four. Céline was dying of cancer; the purpose of our trip was to allow my mother to say farewell to her sister and to spend time with her mother afterward. We would stay in Colombia for a week or two, then go on to Brazil, where *Nonno* and *Nonna* awaited us.

In Bogotá, I was happy to find a houseful of cousins—in New York there were only two—though I had difficulty telling them apart. André, Roget, Claude, Roby, Stella, Myrna, Joyce. The older boys, especially, seemed indistinguishable to me. And I had trouble finding my place among them. Their ways differed from ours, simultaneously wilder and more restrained. At home, they obeyed their strict father without question; away, they let go with greater abandon.

Céline's husband, my *Oncle* Siahou, was a large man, with an explosive temper and a loud laugh. He frightened me, as did his brother, the more familiar *Oncle* Joe in New York, married to my mother's friend Suzanne, whom we called *Tante* Suze. Given to strong Havana cigars—he let them dangle from the side of his mouth—and heavy gold rings, Siahou moved with broad, almost aggressive gestures. *"Laisse-moi te voir,"* he would demand. "Let me look at you"; and he would pull me toward him, his rough hands grasping my small waist, his large eyes peering into mine. *"Elle est jolie,"* he would tell my mother, winking broadly, *"très jolie."* "She's pretty, she's very pretty." Putting his fingers to his lips, he would kiss them with an exaggerated smack: *"Mmm, délicieuse!"*

Because my mother spent her days with Céline and my cousins were in school, I was often left to myself while a servant cared for my brother. Most mornings, I wandered alone on the paths leading up the mountain that rose behind the house.

The pungent scent of eucalyptus enveloped me as I walked beneath the huge trees. Not far from the house a swift stream ran between steep banks; I crossed it on an ancient bridge constructed of dried mud and twigs. No wider than a footpath, perhaps twelve inches thick and twenty feet long, the bridge was a triumph of indigenous engineering—more marvelous to me than any of the Seven Wonders about which I had read on the plane. I held my breath each time I inched my way across, afraid to look down. In the distance, women scrubbed clothes in the running water, spreading white shirts and colored blouses to dry on gray rocks.

My aunt was dying. For the duration of our stay, I saw her out of bed only once, for the wedding of her eldest daughter, Stella. Most days, I would be led for a few minutes into her darkened bedroom, where she lay on a high hospital bed covered in crisp white sheets. Beside her was a white enameled bowl—the bedpan, which my mother or a nurse placed beneath her when necessary. I noticed vials, tubes, towels. No one spoke to me of death, no one said the word "cancer," yet I could see that my aunt was very ill. People whispered at her bedside, as if to hide a secret shame. From time to time my aunt cried, pleading for morphine. I could hear her screams from behind closed doors. But when I was led in to see her, Céline smiled weakly, touched my hair, said she was glad we had come.

Stella's wedding, originally planned for June, had been rescheduled for two months earlier so that Céline might witness her daughter as a bride. During our stay, the house was busy with the preparations—simultaneously hushed for death and noisy in anticipation of marriage. Stella's fiancé brought flowers every day at noon; after lunch, the couple sat together in the living room, fondling one another secretly, kissing when they thought no one was looking. Mornings and afternoons, there were consultations about dresses, flowers, the menu for the reception. Stella was slender, blonde, tall, and, graceful—a storybook bride. Her wedding was held at an ornate Bogotá synagogue; *Tante* Suze and

Oncle Joe flew in from New York; *Tante* Céline, dressed in green silk, sat in a wheelchair, propped up on pillows.

At eight, I understood neither marriage nor mortality, though I knew them to be among the mysteries of adulthood. In that house on the edge of a great city, beside a wild mountain, the scent of eucalyptus mingled for me with the smells of sex and death. Alone, I struggled to distinguish between them, to distill their essences and discern their specific qualities. Confronted with the bodies of my cousin and my aunt—one young, vibrant, strong; the other old, bloated, worn—I became aware in a new way of my own; it seemed weak and vulnerable, unknown. What was my bond to these women? What would it be for me to grow into womanhood? I became awkward in my own skin, self-conscious, heavy. At night I wet my bed—the warm dampness woke me—and my stomach swelled unaccountably.

Once, while I was walking up the mountain with my cousins, one of the boys and I became separated from the larger group. Telling me to be quiet, my cousin pinned me down in the brush beside the path; as I fought against him, I scraped my knee on a rock and began to bleed. I tried shouting as loudly as I could, but no one heard. I screamed, but no one came. My voice vanished in the high canopy, dissolving amid the calls of birds, fading among the bright flowers. When we returned to the house my mother reprimanded me for having dirtied my dress; she found a clean, freshly ironed one, and warned me to be more careful next time. Did my cousin do more than simply hold me down? Was he only playing? My mind balks when I try to press further—but my body, uneasy, tells its tale.

Céline did not die during our stay in Bogotá, which we extended from two to six weeks. Although my mother might have wanted to be present for her sister's death, our round-trip ticket was valid for only three months, and we needed to get to Brazil, to *Nonna*. Céline was in a coma; there was little we could do. Reluctantly, my mother said good-bye, and we departed for São Paulo.

Our small plane flew low over the Andes toward Lima, Peru. The pilot angled the plane until we were flying parallel to the steep mountain slopes, above the vast reaches of Lake Titicaca, the highest lake in the world, glittering blue and still, unmoved by our sputtering presence. In Lima, we spent the night in an old hotel at the center of town. I remember white buildings reflecting bright sun; tall columns; shaded arcades; a dusty square where vendors sold tortillas and sweets. In the morning, we boarded another plane. For eight hours, we flew high above the Amazon jungle; while my mother and brother slept, I strained to see the river below us.

The airport in São Paulo was crowded with relatives—all of them ours, it seemed. In a rush, they surrounded us, kissing, hugging, squeezing, exclaiming. There were *Tante* Diane and her husband, *Oncle* Albert; my *Oncles* Lucien and Eli; my cousins Robbie and André. My cheek was pricked by the sharp stubble of *Oncle* Lucien's beard; I smelled the tobacco on his hands and face, the cologne on his neck. I was pinched and hugged by *Tante* Diane. Her clear-eyed elfin face captivated me; her cheerful voice put me at ease. I gave myself up, allowing *Oncle* Albert to lift me into the air; his brusque voice, sturdy arms, and wide chest promising safety, no matter how high I whirled. Everyone spoke at once—in English, French, Portuguese, Arabic—as we tumbled into cars that sped us to the low-ceilinged apartment where *Nonna* and *Nonno* awaited our arrival.

By the time of that visit in 1958, *Nonna* was close to seventy, in good health but frail, and almost entirely blind. She bore her blindness with grace, her infirmity only adding to her dignity. She would hold out a pale, almost translucent hand and someone would take it, leading her to a chair or to her bed. When we entered the apartment, she felt my face with her fingers, lightly traced the curve of my brows and cheeks and lips. Satisfied, "*C'est Joysica*," she proclaimed, and hugged me to her, a smile on her calm face.

"She never complained," my mother says of this *Nonna*,

contrasting her with the other one. "She taught me never to complain."

Nonna's serenity was manifest in the steadiness of her movements, the gentleness of her voice, the peace with which she sat, silent, amid a busy household. Born into a cosmopolitan Alexandrian family, descended from prosperous Iraqi merchants, she had known comfort, even luxury, in her youth. Her quiet calm may in part have been a legacy of that privilege. But I prefer to believe that her composure was a deliberately cultivated habit she could claim as her own.

With the exception of my *Oncle* Eli, who lived with his Brazilian wife, Anita, on the other side of town, my mother's family in Brazil shared two small apartments in a newly built high-rise, a rectangular tower of poured concrete walls, terrazzo floors, and narrow balconies cut into the facade. *Tante* Diane and *Oncle* Albert and their children lived in one two-bedroom apartment; across the hall was another, shared by *Nonna*, *Nonno*, and my unmarried *Oncle* Lucien. In Cairo, the family had lived in one large apartment, not two small ones; the floors had been marble, not tile; they had had four or five servants, not one. But there had been the same easy camaraderie, the same daily banter and play, the same range of generations living together, the coming and going of men and women and children. It was a life of affectionate teasing, sometimes boisterous conversation, and long, happy meals.

In Brazil, I helped my *Tante* Diane shop for those meals at the *feira*, the open-air market set up each morning in a different section of São Paulo. Twice a week, we left at dawn, carrying paper bags Diane had saved from the week before. Diane confidently led me through the bustling market, hurrying to find the freshest, best produce before it was gone. It wasn't quite like the markets in Cairo, she told me, but it was good. To me, the *feira* was more festival than market, a fantastic gathering of people, produce, textiles, crafts. On another scale entirely from the Italian market in Brooklyn where I shopped with my mother, it occupied a full city block and was filled with rows upon rows of busy stalls. I clung to my aunt, simultaneously fearing I might get lost and longing to dissolve into the crowd.

We returned from the *feira* laden with bags of tantalizing fruits and vegetables, meat, flowers, sometimes even little trinkets for the house. Everyone joined in the process of putting the food away, and then in preparations for the midday meal. Even *Nonna* had a part. My mother would bring her a bowl of potatoes, and, with a paring knife in her right hand, *Nonna* would pick up the potato with her left, feeling its curves and indentations. Slowly, carefully, she would begin to peel, letting a thin brown strip of skin spiral down. When she was finished, my mother would take the peeled potato from her, give her another.

Meals at the apartment in São Paulo were served in an alcove off the small kitchen—at the same table where we gathered to do the cooking. At lunch every day there would be least ten people: *Tante* Diane, *Oncle* Albert, *Oncle* Lucien, *Nonna*, *Nonno*, my mother, my brother, my two cousins, and me. Sometimes *Oncle* Eli would join us along with his wife, Anita. My uncles Lucien and Albert came home every day from their downtown jobs. I sensed that work was difficult for them; only at home could they relax, cosseted by a flock of women. The women served, and the men ate. Afterward, while the men took naps or read the newspaper, the women cleaned up.

Later, after the men had returned to work, the women gathered again, this time in the living room, to talk and to sew. Often we were joined by other friends and relatives—*Tante* Suze's sister Yoli; my mother's girlhood friend Cécile; *Tante* Diane's neighbor from Cairo, Jeanne. Each woman now fingered an article of clothing that needed mending—a shirt without a button, a skirt with a torn hem, pants with unraveled seams. Diane would give *Nonna* a worn sock, threading a thick needle for her. Placing the sock on a wooden darning egg, *Nonna* felt for the hole with her keen fingertips, then slowly began to weave across the gap, filling it in closely. As the women stitched, they talked in gentle voices about marriages and births, illnesses and deaths, engagements and bar mitzvahs. They spoke mostly in French, though, for my aunt Anita's sake, they sometimes used Portuguese, and when they didn't want me to understand, Arabic.

Instead of being asked to mend, I was given a tablecloth to embroider, a simple pattern of green and red cross-stitching. Later, I was entrusted with a more complex design: a spotted fawn amid fanciful flowers. *Tante* Diane had led me through narrow São Paulo streets to a shop where we selected the pattern and purchased skeins of silky, luminous cotton thread. Diane taught me the simple stitches I would need: the prosaic chain stitch for all the outlines, the elegant French knot for eyes and the hearts of flowers, the lovely smooth satin stitch for the bright spots on the fawn. Eagerly, I bent to my task, happy to be included among the women.

I didn't realize it then, but during that month in São Paulo, I tasted briefly the life I might have known had our family remained in Cairo, had there been no further conflicts between Jews and Arabs. It was, essentially, a tribal life, communal, governed entirely by the custom of rigid separation between male and female lives and work and an equally rigid separation from the larger society within which we all lived. The men went out every day into a world figured as alien and hostile; the women labored at home to create a welcoming sanctuary, an inner realm of familiarity and comfort. Women's only ventures out were to shop or to visit one another in equally familiar homes. At the age of eight, I was entranced by this ancient arrangement.

I would have another reaction when I returned four years later, by then a *jeune fille*, a young girl, no longer *un enfant*, a child. This time I was impatient with the women in their narrow domestic circle; I wanted to be among the men, forging a path through the outer world. And it was just then that my first menstrual period arrived, marking me as definitively female. *Nonna* brusquely slapped my cheek when she was told. It was the custom, my mother said, this is how girls are welcomed into womanhood. My cheek burned and my eyes teared. I didn't want this welcome, I wanted to say, I didn't want this life. But already I could hear the whispers: *"Aroosa,"* the women were saying. *"In sha'allah aroosa,"* "May you be a bride, God willing."

◆

For one glorious week during that first visit in 1958, my mother, my brother, my aunt, my cousins, and I took a beach holiday in Santos. The bus from São Paulo swept us down to the sea, depositing us at an old wooden hotel with wide verandahs at one end of a curving bay. *"Ça rappele la Corniche à Alexandrie, n'est-ce pas?"* my aunt said to my mother, remembering the wide promenade that stretched along the Mediterranean in the city where they had spent their childhood summers. "It's reminiscent of the Corniche in Alexandria, isn't it?"

That week at Santos stands out as among the most perfect moments of my childhood, a true vacation, after which I would model all my later ones. On the one hand, I felt remarkably grown up, staying in a hotel, eating in a great dining room where I was served by waiters in black jackets; on the other, I was free to be fully a child, instead of the responsible young person I had already become. At Santos, thanks largely to *Tante* Diane, I was completely indulged: if I wanted an ice cream cone I got one; if I wanted to stay on the beach until dusk, I was allowed to. For my mother and her sister, too, that week must have been an extraordinary gift, a happy interlude in lives scarred by separation and loss. During their own childhood, they had spent long summers at the beach. Leaving her husband behind in Cairo, *Nonna* would take the children to her mother's house beside the sea in Alexandria. Later, during the war, the family would go to Ras al-Bar, a sandbar in the Nile Delta. Flooded annually, Ras al-Bar was the most magical of beach resorts. Houses were constructed of bamboo mats hung from metal frames. At the end of each season, the mats were rolled up and stored away. Like the airy houses, life at Ras al-Bar had an improvised, light quality, set apart from the rigid proprieties of middle-class Jewish life in Cairo. At Ras al-Bar, the world was populated almost entirely by women and children, free to laugh and play on the sand and in the sea.

So, for the two sisters Diane and Nelly, this vacation at Santos must have been a sweet reprise. While they could not forget Céline, their older sister, dying in Bogotá, for the moment, they could relax, breathing the salt air, stretching their limbs in the sea, letting the sun warm their own strong bodies. When we returned to São Paulo, the idyll was over.

The telegram came in the afternoon. My brother and I were in Diane's living room, along with my mother, Diane, and *Nonna*. *Nonna*'s shriek pierced the stillness; I saw her blind hands reach for the slip of paper my aunt had let fall, watched her mouth open and close silently, as she began to rock, to pull at her hair. "Non," she cried, "*non, non, non. Ça aurait du être moi, pas ma fille. Ça devrait être moi.*" "It should have been me, not my daughter, it should have been me."

Nonna raged against this death, a daughter taken before a mother. She had lost a son fifteen years earlier, but this loss, of her eldest daughter, the one she loved the most, was worse. Her grief mounted: She beat her chest and face, ripped her dress, begged to be taken in death herself. Seeking to shield us, my mother took my brother and me into the kitchen. But I had already seen the worst—my grandmother undone, my beloved *Nonna* fierce with grief. Diane led *Nonna* into her own apartment, where *Nonno* might console her. I could still hear her cries through the walls, echoing through the hall. They tore at me, leaving me desolate as well. We had come to South America for this, to be present when *Nonna* received the news of Céline's death, but the immensity of the moment crushed us all. For the rest of our stay, *Nonna* was gone from us, abandoned to her grief. Without her, we were left to grope alone, lost in a world suddenly grown dark.

◆

Nonna's husband, *Nonno*, like all the men in our family, was a distant figure, dwelling in a world apart. Yet among the men, he was the one who offered me the greatest intimacy. Like *Nonna*, he had in his old age acquired a sweet docility. I was eager to sit on his knees, to hold his hand, to look into his bright eyes.

Born into a large Aleppo family, *Nonno* had come to Cairo when he was one year old ("just like you coming to America," my mother reminds me). As an adult, he imported textiles from England, though he had also speculated in stocks. When the market crashed in 1929, he opened a private casino in Cairo, *Le Club des Familles*, where Jewish men came with their wives to play cards and gamble. *Nonna* prepared and served pastries while *Nonno* socialized with his patrons. Several times a year, *Nonno* took long, solitary trips to Europe, "for business I guess," my mother says, though she also recalls that he took the waters at Vichy and Baden, coming home with expensive Italian suits and ties, fine leather shoes.

The man I got to know in Brazil still dressed with care each morning, putting on suspenders, a tie, a crisply ironed shirt, an immaculate suit, matching socks, and polished shoes—even if he was not planning to go out. His large, intelligent eyes smiled at me from behind tiny, wire-framed glasses; he was nearly bald and he had a beige plastic hearing aid in one ear. *Nonna* was blind and *Nonno* was deaf. The distribution of my grandparents' infirmities intrigued me. I thought of my grandparents as a complementary pair, together making a complete whole: I imagined that *Nonno* would tell *Nonna* what he saw while she repeated to him what she heard. In fact, isolated from one another as they were for most of every day, my grandparents dwelt in separate worlds, *Nonna* smiling at visions only she could see, *Nonno* nodding to music only he could hear.

To stay busy now, *Nonno* collected stamps, a hobby he had refined into an art. Every day, while the women cooked or cleaned or sewed, and the younger men went to their jobs, *Nonno* sat alone at his desk in the room he shared with *Nonna*. The desk, an old rolltop with a multitude of small compartments and drawers, was pushed against the wall between their two single beds. On good days, I would be invited to join him.

Nonno's stamp collection was arranged, not in preprinted albums, but in individually labeled, spiral-bound *"Cadernos Escolars,"* lined school notebooks he purchased at local stationery stores. *Nonno* knew, from studying various manuals and indexes, exactly which stamps had been issued by which country and when. His objective was to accumulate and display a full series of each stamp, and he carefully laid out the spaces in his books, using a ruler and pencil, leaving gaps for the stamps he was confident would eventually turn up. He numbered each page and wrote out a detailed table of contents on the first page of each book: Algeria, Angola, Argentina; Belgium, Bolivia, Bulgaria; Chile, Croatia, Czechoslovakia.

Working slowly, patiently, he demonstrated his techniques for me. Stamps still on envelopes would be soaked briefly in shallow bowls of water until they could be slipped off. Grasping them with tweezers, *Nonno* removed the stamps from the envelopes, then laid them to dry on clean white sheets of paper. Once dried, the stamps would be sorted, first by country, then by series, then by date, denomination, color. *Nonno* worked methodically, examining each stamp through a large magnifying glass to ascertain its details and condition. *"Regarde,"* he said proudly, *"regarde comme ils sont beaux!"* "Look, see how beautiful they are!" To affix the stamps to his notebook pages, *Nonno* used tiny gummed cellophane hinges he bought in packages from the stationer's; but because he thought them unnecessarily large, he cut each hinge in half before using it.

Friends and relatives, apprised of *Nonno*'s hobby, saved stamps for him. At home in Brooklyn, we carefully preserved the stamps that brought the mail from Israel or England or France or Egypt; my mother cut the corners of the envelopes, put them in a drawer, then included them in her monthly letters to Brazil. But *Nonno* rarely kept the stamps he received from thoughtful relatives: They were only a sort of lagniappe, providing the means for him to trade. His major source of usable stamps were the weekly trading sessions he attended in a São Paulo park.

Sunday mornings, while most of the city slept, *Nonno* rose early for his long trek; he had to take two or three buses to reach the shady park where other elderly men had set up small tables to exhibit their stamps. A few times during our visit, I was allowed to accompany him on the long, quiet bus rides. At the park, stamps were laid out in tantalizing displays, some in envelopes, some already sorted, some simply in a jumble. *Nonno* would walk around, casually chatting and joking, looking over what was available. He would bring out his own stamps, showing them to another collector, proudly demonstrating their worth. Quietly, steadily, deals would be made. We arrived home laden with new treasures, ready for another afternoon of soaking and sorting and placing.

While we were in Brazil, *Nonno* set up several notebooks for me and gave me hundreds of stamps so that I could begin my own collection. But the hobby never took. I was too restless, unable to cultivate the necessary patience. For many years, the notebooks remained hidden in a box in a closet; recently, I retrieved them, placing them on a shelf near my writing desk. Occasionally now, I leaf through these yellowing books, admiring the delicacy of my grandfather's handwriting, intrigued by the finely drawn and beautifully colored illustrations of unknown kings and queens, ancient cathedrals and temples, modern skyscrapers, palm trees, elephants, kangaroos, birds. Studying a nation's stamps, I begin to see, one can intuit its history, make guesses about its values and beliefs. I examine the section for Egypt. The oldest stamps, marked *"postes d'Egypte,"* are adorned with detailed line drawings of mosques, pyramids, the king. Later, the nation's name is written in English, "Egypt," and the proportion of Arabic writing increases: I discern *"Misr"* in Arabic characters, "UAR" in bright red. The bold graphics now emphasize industry, defense, trade, and transportation: There are oil derricks, pipelines, soldiers, cars, trains, planes, and new hotels.

Inside the notebooks, I find envelopes addressed to me, "Mlle Joyce Zonana," in my grandfather's frail hand. These are filled with more stamps, unsorted treasures my grandfather selected. I become ashamed of my neglect, sorry for all the chances I have missed. Lately, I find myself unwilling to throw away the stamps that bring my mail from abroad. A personal or business letter will come to me from England or Holland or Greece, and I will be struck by the bright bit of color, delighted by a strange new image. And then, almost involuntarily, I will tear off the corner before throwing away the envelope, place it in a desk drawer where other bits of envelopes accumulate. I dream that one day I will find the time, that I will spend long, leisurely hours in contemplation and discovery. I will catalogue the stamps I have; I will display them; I will make arrangements to get the others that are missing.

Stamps call to me now—and perhaps they called to my grandfather for the same reason—because they embody, in their wonderfully delicate and evanescent forms, the steady efforts people have made to stay in touch, defying time and distance, political change, religious struggle. These days, I keep up with my Israeli cousins by e-mail; I speak regularly with my brother on our cell phones; I fly often to visit friends. Yet letters still provide for me the most satisfying medium of communication. Even when they are typed or printed out by computer, I savor the traces left on them by my correspondents; I treasure the revelations brought by the written word. When I travel, even for brief vacations, I send scores of postcards to my friends: Nothing pleases me more than to get a letter from someone I imagined had vanished from my life.

When they were first separated—after the waves of departures from Cairo—my relatives kept in touch *par avion, via correo aero*, via air mail—using the light-weight blue envelopes and rustling thin paper that allowed them to narrate complex histories for the price of one stamp. My mother wrote in a miniscule, cramped hand, filling two sides of the almost transparent sheets all the way to the edges, leaving no margins. Letters arrived from Egypt and Colombia and then Brazil equally brimming: stories about *les enfants* interspersed with details about work and health and finances. In closing, there would be a multitude of kisses, "*des baisers*," along with generous "*souhaits de bonne chance*," wishes for good luck—a world, a life, rendered palpable through the written word, transmitted across continents with the aid of stamps, those fragile bearers of relation.

Five: Yom Tov

◆ ◆ ◆

For more than ten years during the late 1950s and early 1960s, my father wrote every few months from our home in Brooklyn to the Egyptian Ministry of Finance in Cairo, seeking to obtain his pension. He was certain he was entitled to

Felix Zonana, at home in Florida, 1990s.

it, having worked in the civil service there for nearly twenty years. Unlike most Jews who had lived in Cairo and Alexandria during the early part of the twentieth century, he was an Egyptian citizen, and he retained that status even after being naturalized in the United States. So he could see no reason for Nasser's government to deny his claim, and he persisted despite the bureaucratic resistance he encountered. Although it took months for each letter to be answered, he calmly waited for the official response, then carefully drafted a reply in Arabic. His was a long, steady, determined campaign. When the refusals or evasions arrived, he never became angry or impatient; he simply wrote another letter. In time, his protracted effort bore fruit: for the last years of his life, he received his pension on a more-or-less quarterly basis. The checks, drawn on the Bank of Egypt, were for less than $150 each; my father's name was usually misspelled; and the numbers in his Florida address were often transposed. But his sense of justice had been assuaged. "It's the principle," he told me when I protested once that the money wouldn't amount to much. *"C'est le principe."*

Clarity of accounts, fastidious precision in all his affairs, characterized my father. "Your father is such an old-fashioned gentleman," social workers in the senior day care center would tell me when I came by with my mother to pick him up. "He always has a kind word for everybody." Barely able to move, often unaware of where he was and to whom he was speaking, my father still tried to tip his hat—in those last days, a soft, beige or white cotton cap—when greeting a woman; he extended his hand toward each man he encountered. He would fret if he failed properly to say good-bye to someone; he felt keenly the limitations of his Parkinson's disease and was distressed when he could not follow the forms of etiquette.

"Should I give her some money?" he asked me once when I left him sitting beside my partner while my mother and I went for a swim. He was disoriented by the unaccustomed drive to a beachside motel and didn't recognize Kay, thinking she was perhaps an employee of the place. "No," I tried to reassure him, "that's Kay, and she wants to be with you." But he remained confused, kept searching for some change to offer her, uncomfortable accepting care from someone he imagined was a stranger.

Parkinson's took much from my father. At the end, he could neither move nor speak easily, he could no longer read or write, and the clarity of his thinking was often compromised. He needed to depend on others for help with his most basic bodily functions—eating, eliminating, bathing. But his greatest loss, I believe, was his ability to perform the ritual of morning prayer that centered his life for more than sixty-five years, ever since his bar mitzvah. Until Parkinson's made it impossible for him to stand or to read, every day, before breakfast and after shaving, he intoned in Hebrew the prayer required of all Jewish men. Every day, he spent nearly half an hour fulfilling this obligation—precious time he set aside no matter how long his commute on the crowded subway, no matter how many extra hours he had worked the night before.

My father was the only member of our household with any formal religious practice. My mother, despite her attention to the details of setting the holiday table and her vague sense of a benevolent spirit in nature, had no serious engagement with Judaism; my paternal grandmother had no faith or piety that I could discern; and for the longest time both my brother and I were ignorant of the most basic tenets of Judaism. Although my father was raised an Orthodox Jew and went when he could to an Orthodox synagogue in Brooklyn, his commitment to morning prayer was the only overt sign of his orthodoxy. Unlike most of our Jewish neighbors, we neither observed the Sabbath nor kept kosher. Although we celebrated each major holiday (*yom tov* or "good day," Rosh Hashanah, Hanukkah, and Pesach) in great style, and offered blessings over wine and bread on Friday nights (we used pita not challah), we had no ongoing experience of Judaism as a living religion. My brother eventually mastered enough Hebrew to recite at his bar mitzvah, but I was taught nothing. Whatever I knew of faith I learned by watching my father.

Every morning, as I engaged in my own daily rituals—making the family's beds, setting the breakfast table, gathering up my school things—I would steal glimpses of my father, still in his striped cotton pajamas, methodically preparing to pray. He would stand in the center of the living room, the only clear space in the apartment, and take his white satin yarmulke from the top left drawer of the heavy mahogany bureau. From the same drawer, he removed the gilt-embroidered blue velvet pouch in which he kept his ancient siddur, a faded red leather prayer book; his tallith, a fringed silk prayer shawl; and his tefillin, the black leather phylacteries Jewish men are enjoined to wrap around their arms and foreheads. ("And thou shalt bind them for a sign upon thy hands and they shall be for frontlets between thine eyes.")

Facing the east—with his back to the windows—he would gently kiss the siddur, letting it fall open to the accustomed page: he had been using the same siddur, tallith, and tefillin since his bar mitzvah in 1926. (He had been eleven and a half, not thirteen, for the ceremony initiating a Jewish boy into the obligations and privileges of manhood; the rabbi judged that, as an "orphan," he should begin saying kaddish for his father.) The ritual objects had accompanied him across the Atlantic, and now, no matter how worn they became—the siddur, in particular, was especially fragile, with loose and crumbling yellow pages and a front cover that had separated from its binding—he clung to them stubbornly. Periodically my mother would offer to buy him a new tallith, but he always refused.

And it was this worn ivory-colored silk tallith, frayed yet shining, that he carefully unfolded each morning. After putting on his yarmulke, he would drape the tallith across his shoulders, examining and kissing the fringes, then pulling it over his head. "I am here enwrapping my body in the fringed robe," he would say quietly in Hebrew, "so shall my soul . . . be enwrapped in the light of the fringes." The Sephardic liturgy describes the prayer shawl in rich metaphors of luminous power. Likened to a maternal eagle sheltering her young, it is also a garment of light, like the curtain God spreads in the heavens. As my father let the gleaming shawl embrace him, it clung to him intimately, like a lover, spiriting him away from our everyday tumult.

Enfolding himself in the tallith marked only the beginning of my father's entrance into prayer. Next came the binding of the tefillin, the small leather boxes containing fragments of Hebrew scripture. Each box was attached to long black strips of worn leather; one was affixed to the forehead and one to the arm. Kissing each one, my father wrapped the leather first around his forehead, then wound it seven times around his left arm—like the oil of goodness, the siddur says, that God pours into the seven lamps of creation. Finally, he coiled the end of the strap three times around his middle finger:

> *And I will betroth thee unto me for ever; yea, I will betroth thee unto me in righteousness, and in judgment, and in lovingkindness, and in mercy; I will even betroth thee unto me in faithfulness; and thou shalt know the Lord.*

I did not know then what my father said as he wrapped himself with the tefillin, and I doubt whether he even paused to contemplate the significance of the ancient Hebrew words he repeated so faithfully. But the physical rite alone carried meaning: As he wound the tefillin, he was uniting himself fully, in a ceremony of solemn betrothal, to the God whose greatness enveloped him. Veiled and encircled, he became a sort of bride, God's humble *aroosa*. The tefillin—placed opposite his heart and against his forehead—marked the all-encompassing nature of this relationship: "And thou shalt love the Lord thy God with all thine heart, and with all thy soul, and with all thy might." Watching from my corner with rapt attention, I too was bound, seized by my father's devotion, entering into my own solemn relationship with something I could not name.

My father never spoke to us about his morning ritual—what it meant to him, why he did it; he never told us anything at all about the God he worshipped. We did not talk about the things that mattered most: God, sex, death. There was a kind of tact in this silence, a fitting reverence for mysteries that transcend language. In Hebrew, the name of God must not—indeed cannot—be written; it is unutterable. The sacred is the unspeakable, the ineffable. It is "hidden," as one cabbalist writes, "like the taste of food, which is impossible to describe to one who has never tasted it." Once, in my twenties, I asked my mother why she had never talked with me about sex—had she been ashamed? I wondered. "No," she confessed, there was no shame. "It's just that it was so powerful, so important. I didn't know how to talk about it." So it must have been for my father and his God.

Yet the silence of our household was also a great loss, condemning each of us to solitude despite our cramped intimacy. The things we didn't talk about grew in power: If they seemed holy, they also seemed sinful, the greatest blessing or the greatest curse. Language itself became both sacrament and sacrilege, encircled by a taboo that stops me even now as I risk these words. I seem to myself a profane trespasser, crudely violating the sanctity of the unspoken. I fear I will be stricken, maimed—if I get things wrong, or, worse, if I get them right.

As a child I could see that it was language—and most especially written language, the beautifully calligraphed and mysterious Hebrew language—that brought my father into contact with God. Hebrew words and letters were themselves numinous, charged with power: Even unread, wound into the tight parchment scrolls we placed on our doorjambs or over our hearts, these words had the power to transform. My father would kiss the Hebrew words enfolded into a mezzuzzah as he entered and exited the house; I was told I could kiss the tiny silver mezzuzzah around my neck any time I needed help.

I wanted to learn those words too, to participate in the

mystery. I begged my parents to send me to Hebrew school, so that I might acquire the secrets of those curling black letters that danced through the pages of my father's siddur. My parents refused: There was no money to spare, and, besides, it was a man's duty and privilege to communicate with God, not a woman's. My brother, who did not share my longing, studied Hebrew in my stead. When, many years later, I summoned the courage to begin lessons at a New Orleans synagogue, I found myself sobbing as I sounded out my first words, actually reading for the first time the central Jewish affirmation of faith. *"Shema, Yisrael, Adonai Elohenu, Adonai Ehod,"* I said aloud with the woman teacher—"Hear O Israel, the Lord our God, the Lord is One"—and I saw refracted in my tears the shining tenfold light of the sefirot, the shimmering radiance with which my father clothed himself each day.

◆

That light was at its brightest every year at Passover, when, at a long table gleaming with crystal and newly polished silver, my father led the prayer from the Haggadah, the Passover liturgy. He was joined by a group of other men (his brother Isaac and his cousin Edward; *Oncle* Joe perhaps; and an old friend from Cairo, a solitary lawyer named Gabriel). The men's wives and children—more than twenty people in all most years—were also there to celebrate with us. Folding tables and chairs were brought out from the closet; there was barely room to walk around them. The ritual holiday foods were dramatically arranged in silver platters on white damask cloths: crisp green lettuce and chicory, hard-boiled eggs, a lamb shank, matzo, a thick *charoseth* made from dates, wine, and hazelnuts. The Hebrew words of blessing would transform them all: *Charoseth* would become the mortar used in building the pyramids; chicory, the bitter tears the enslaved Hebrews shed for their suffering; the lamb, the children who were sacrificed—or spared—by God's wrath.

Numerous copies of the Haggadah were scattered on the

tables—some, colorfully illustrated commercial pamphlets printed by kosher wine companies; others, bare booklets mimeographed by local synagogues. I would search for the most comprehensive translation, trying to match its meager English to the rich Hebrew the men chanted. Too often, whole sections were omitted; it was difficult to find my place as the men raced through the service. Vainly I would ask them to slow down, begging for full explanations. But the pressure of the long ceremony, the cries of the younger children waiting for dinner, the gossip and laughter of the older women, drowned out my pleas.

From time to time, though, I managed to read aloud in English a passage of my own choosing. My favorite was the one detailing the efforts of scholars to ascertain the total number of plagues. Reasoning from the fact that the biblical text asserts that God's "finger" was on the land, while his "hand" was stretched over the sea, one commentator argues that, if there were 10 plagues on the land, there were forty on the sea. A later commentator suggests that the number on the sea should be fifty, since a hand is five times larger than a finger. Finally, Rabbi Ben Zoma asserts that there were fifty plagues on land and 250 on the sea, for each plague was manifold, containing a variety of God's qualities: wrath, anger, awesome power, might, and glory. I loved the arcane logic of these disputes, and I read the passage aloud with grand flourishes, pointing my finger, extending my hand, winning the laughter of the men who paused to watch my performance.

More serious, and more frightening, was the moment in the reading when the plagues themselves were represented. As my father enumerated the horrors, using the Hebrew words, he would dip his finger into his cup of wine, then shake it into a basin of water my mother held behind him.

"*Dam*"—blood
"*Tzfardeyah*"—frogs
"*Kinim*"—lice

"Arov"—swarms
"Dever"—blight

For each drop of wine—was it wine or blood I wondered—that fell from my father's finger, my mother poured water into the bowl from a pitcher. The terrifying enumeration continued:

"Sh'chin"—boils
"Barad"—hail
"Arbeh"—locusts
"Choshech"—darkness
"Makat B'chorot"—slaying of the first born

Neither my father nor my mother looked at the basin, and none of us at the table was supposed to look either. We sat with eyes averted, sensing but not seeing the terrible drama enacting itself at our table. At those moments, I was sure that if I were to look, I would in fact see God; I would see and be destroyed by the plagues, in all their overwhelming power.

Because I knew that the story of Passover was especially meaningful for us, I made an effort, every year, to open myself to its full significance. The subject, I knew, was the exodus of the Jews from Egypt, their long-awaited deliverance from slavery. The holiday commemorates a moment of miraculous transformation, the stunning and instantaneous shift from bad fortune to good, from bondage to freedom. It demonstrates that there is order in the universe, that God can and will set things right. "In every generation," the Haggadah enjoins, "each of us should feel as though we ourselves had personally gone forth from Egypt." But for us there need be no "as though." We *had* personally gone forth from Egypt, and I reveled in this chance to experience our distinctive status. Our lives confirmed the truth of the ancient text. Passover was our special holiday, for in our experience the figurative—*as though*—had become literal—*in fact*. Yet I also knew that the Egypt from which the ancient Jews departed was a place of oppression and pain, while for our family, Egypt had been a land of sunshine and ease. It was hard to reconcile these two images, and I wonder if it wasn't because of the Passover ritual that I had such a difficult time returning to Cairo: I did not know where I would be going, unable to grasp the particularity of Egypt, a place that was to me as much symbol as reality in all its different names—the *Mizraim* of Jewish tradition, the *Misr* of contemporary national politics, or the lost colonial *Egypte* of my parents' still-bright dreams.

◆

The annual Passover service, with its practice of convivial commentary on a revered text, imprinted me with a passion for midrash, for literary discussion and interpretation. All the seminars I later attended and eventually conducted were but pale replicas of those glorious feasts where the word shimmered, elusive, just beyond my grasp. When, these days, I lead a discussion in a literature class, I know that I have cast myself in my father's place. The texts I use are secular, not sacred, the words in a language I imagine I understand. But along with my students I search for meaning all the same, trying first one interpretation, then another, seeking to make sense of a design that promises at best deliverance, at worst a pleasant diversion. Reading the same texts over and over again, I work to do what my father has done, though, like him, I am often surrounded by people who would rather hurry up and get to the meal. It would be more satisfying, I sometimes think, to wrap myself in a tallith, bind the tefillin upon my arm, give myself over to solitary prayer.

◆

During the last years of his life, my father took his prescribed pills with the same regularity with which he once performed the mitzvah of daily prayer: a red one and two blue ones in the morning, two yellow ones and a white one at noon, a small white one and a large red one at night. He was on Symmetrel and Elavil and Depranil, each providing a portion of the brain chemicals necessary for a semblance of emotional stability, cognitive clarity, and physical dexterity. I wonder if the ritual of prayer wouldn't have served him more reliably.

My father was always a vulnerable, fragile man. Without his morning prayer, and the other, more secular rituals upon which he relied—a daily breakfast of cornflakes and bananas; reading the *New York Times* on the subway ride to lower Manhattan; a boiled artichoke for lunch—I imagine he might have been entirely unmoored, without ballast. As it was, he succumbed often to illnesses, enduring several long hospital stays during our first years in the United States and later a "nervous breakdown" that left him permanently weakened. My father was never a strong presence in our home; during his illnesses, he became terrifyingly absent.

The first hospitalizations occurred when I was four, just after we had moved from the security of Mrs. Rosenblum's house to our apartment in the Shore Haven housing complex. My memory of that time is dim, so I turn to my mother for help. First my father had back problems, she says, then he had cancer on his chest.

"He spent six months in bed because of his back," she tells me. "The pain from his disk was so bad that he could not walk. And I was pregnant with your brother."

"But how did we manage?" I ask. "Where did we get the money?"

"The bank where he worked as a clerk gave him sick pay," my mother recalls, "full pay for six months. I didn't know if he would be able to work again; I didn't know if he would live. What was I going to do?"

Twice my father was hospitalized and put in traction, but the debilitating pain in his lower back was not relieved. So my mother took him to a renowned New York specialist who had pioneered a new kind of surgery to heal ruptured disks. *"Les grands docteurs peuvent être très bien,"* she tells me. "The best doctors can sometimes be very good people." She told the doctor we were poor, with one child at home and another obviously on the way. He offered to try his technique on my father, never asking to be paid more than what the insurance company authorized. The experimental operation lasted more than eight hours; within a few days, my father was walking again. Then, a few weeks later my mother became concerned about an abnormal growth on his chest; the biopsy indicated melanoma. Again, my father was hospitalized, this time for three weeks. The surgeon removed several layers of skin, using a graft from his thigh to cover the broad, inch-deep cavity left at the center of his chest.

As when she was pregnant with me, my mother had been advised to stay off her feet to prevent a miscarriage. With my mother in bed much of the time and my father in the hospital or recuperating at home, I had new freedoms—and new responsibilities. Almost every day, I walked alone to the neighborhood supermarket at the end of our long street. The dimly lit store smelled sweet—the floor was swept regularly with sawdust—and the kindly women cashiers welcomed me, helping me count out my change and checking my selections against my mother's list.

I shopped for my mother, but who cooked? Who bathed me and dressed me and cleaned the house? In Egypt, of course, there would have been help—an array of aunts, uncles, grandparents. But in our Brooklyn apartment building, with neighbors above, below, and beside us, there was no one to turn to. For a while, my mother managed by herself, but eventually she had to send me to Manhattan, to stay with *Tante* Suze. For several weeks, I shaped myself to the rhythms of that household, conforming to the rules and tastes of my mother's wealthy friend. Toward the end of the pregnancy, we *all* went to stay with Suze—my mother, my father, and me. When we returned to Brooklyn, I had a brother.

◆

Exactly when my father had his "breakdown"—and what exactly occurred—remains a mystery. "After your brother was born," my mother says, sure of that fact. But she cannot say whether it was before or after *Nonna* came to live with us, before or after our trip to South America. She knows that it was after my father left the bank to take a better-paying position with a small import-export company—even though he felt guilty about leaving the bank that had been so good to him during his long illness. But what year it was she cannot determine. And I cannot place the event at all. For the longest time, I had no conscious knowledge of this crucial moment in our family's history—nothing but a fragmentary image I thought had come to me in a dream:

> In a bare, darkened room, my father lies in bed, covered with heavy blankets. I am brought in to say hello. There are others around us, eager, waiting for our greeting. We have not seen each other in a while. But my father seems not to know me; he cannot remember my name and he does not realize I am his daughter. My mother encourages him: "C'est Joyce, ta fille," she says. "It's Joyce, your daughter." But there is not a glimmer of response. For a moment, I begin to doubt my own existence. Desperate, I try to capture my father's attention, but he remains blank. "Who are you?" he asks, "Why are you here?" My mother leads me away.

For many years, I believed that this scene expressed a truth, but I imagined it to be a metaphor, a symbolic version of my father's distance from me, not an actual event. Still, the fragment had a strong sensory quality, and it persisted, cast up again and again in my awareness like a sealed bottle tossed by the sea. My father's illness was never named; my mother never spoke of those days when he had huddled in the bedroom crying, talking of suicide, unable to get up to go to work. And I knew better than to mention my phantom memory.

It was not until I was in my twenties, visiting *Tante* Suze in

Connecticut, that a chance word suddenly uncorked the past, releasing the truth, now metamorphosed into a towering genie, aroused after a long imprisonment. My mother's friend, whom I called "*tante*," had been chastising me for the pain I had caused my mother, reminding me how much my mother had suffered through the years. I was listening absently, dozing in the sun, trying to distance myself from the familiar litany. Casually, Suze referred to my mother's fear when my father was undergoing shock treatment.

"Shock treatment?" I asked, suddenly rousing myself.

"Yes, of course, shock treatment," Suze went on. "When he had his nervous breakdown."

"What breakdown?" I had to ask again, blinking in the light. "What breakdown, when?"

"Don't tell me you don't know about his breakdown. When you were eight or nine, right after *Nonna* came to live with you. It was a terrible time."

Tante Suze's words were simultaneously dreadful and reassuring. My father had had a "nervous breakdown," whatever that might be. So I had not imagined the scene of his absence. He *had* in fact failed to recognize me, suffering from the temporary amnesia caused by shock treatment. It was he, not I, whose identity had been compromised.

With effort now, as I work to reconstruct the past for this narrative, I persuade my mother to recount the details.

"I had to hide his razors and take all the pills," she says. "He was having a problem with his boss at work, a woman boss, and he became very depressed. I took him to the doctor. He recommended shock treatment. I don't know how many times— maybe for five or six weeks, a few times a week. No, he was never hospitalized. No, he never had psychotherapy. They gave him some drugs, too. We didn't know about these things. He had to get back to work."

My mother does not want to think back to those days, and I hesitate to push her too far. But I try to imagine my father's condition. The closest I can come is my memory of my own episodes of depression, the months and even years when I didn't want to get out of bed in the morning, when it frightened me to dress and walk out the door. From the age of eighteen, I have seen a variety of therapists, tried every technique I could find, but the fragility of my being remains, a vulnerability that seems intractable. Writing these pages, I reenter the old abyss, wander the same labyrinth where my father became lost. The tenuous thread of language holds me, the thin line of words I unreel and then carefully rewind, leading myself back to the light. But at the heart of the maze the monster still lives. My brother, who suffers in the same way, tells me that Sephardic Jews are prone to depression, that it is a genetic predisposition, exacerbated by our custom of intermarriage. I wonder. Might it not also have something to do with the shape of our lives, with our recurring experiences of dislocation and change, our failure ever to settle fully into a permanent home?

Twice as an adult I have seen my father in states that approximated that first descent: once, when he was diagnosed with Parkinson's not long after his retirement, and a second time when he had a surgery to repair again the disk that had ruptured in the 1950s. Parkinson's crept up on my father, causing tremors and occasional blackouts. The family doctor had mentioned the possibility of Parkinson's to my mother, but together they decided to withhold the diagnosis from my father. "Why make him worry?" my mother asked. So, as his symptoms increased and he was told there was nothing wrong, he began to doubt his own perceptions. He grew frightened, spending days at a time crying in bed.

My brother and I had come to New York for the Jewish holiday of Rosh Hashanah, the new year. Victor had flown in from San Francisco, and I was back from Oklahoma, where I had just started my first full-time teaching job. Together, we convinced our mother that our father needed to see a neurologist, to be properly treated for the disease he evidently had. Victor decided to stay a few extra days in New York, to make the appointments and learn what the doctor might say. The morning I left, I went to kiss my father good-bye. He lay in bed, unwilling to get up, in tears, upset that my brother might jeopardize his job by spending these extra days in New York.

A few years later, the Parkinson's already much advanced, my mother decided it was time for them to move to Florida, leaving behind New York's harsh winters. The week before their move, my father's back suddenly flared up with pain that made it impossible for him to walk. Taking a week off from work, I flew to New York to be with him after the surgery. He was desolate, wanting to die, refusing to walk, as the doctors insisted he must. My brother and I lifted him up, walked him slowly through the corridors of the hospital, made efforts to cheer him with talk of our lives.

During his final months, my father often failed to recognize people in the room with him. At times he imagined himself talking to his older brother, Isaac, dead for almost ten years; he thought he was back in Cairo, or working for the small ship-chartering company that had employed him in New York. Often, he would think he was about to go on a journey: He wanted to have his bags ready, the tickets and passports in order. But always, though he sometimes did not know his interlocutor, he remained himself—himself at another moment in time or space, but himself nevertheless. For that brief period in the late 1950s, it seems that he was not himself. How long did the temporary amnesia caused by the shock treatments last? What did he feel when he regained awareness? Was he happy to find himself among us, in a small apartment in Brooklyn? Or did he want to hurry back, back to that dark place where only a blinding jolt of energy could reach him, burning with the force of a brute god?

◆

Both before and after the breakdown, my father worked long hours—nine to five or six on weekdays, and occasionally on weekends at well. He left the house at 7:30 a.m. and returned at 7:30 p.m. Occasionally, he brought home extra work—English/Arabic translations he contracted to do on a per-word basis for Berlitz or a small independent agency. Those moments were great treats for me; he would spread his papers on the dining table and I would sit beside him, as absorbed as he in his quest to find the right word. It didn't matter that I knew no Arabic: I served as his consultant on English idioms, offering my opinions whenever he asked.

Most of the time when he was home, though, my mother told us that he was either sick, *malade*, or tired, *fatigué*. We needed to let him rest, to not trouble him with our demands. We rarely saw him, rarely spent time playing or even talking. Yet there was one special place where my father and I contrived to meet: watching *The Twilight Zone*. Because it was broadcast on Friday nights after my bedtime, I had to obtain special permission to stay up to watch it. My mother was always reluctant, fearing that the show would upset me. But I would turn to my father and ask him to intercede. Like guilty children, then, we would turn on the TV, adjust the picture, and eagerly anticipate the opening chords and the solemn voice of Rod Serling announcing our entrance into the Twilight Zone.

Together, my father and I wandered through that world, a world where solitary men took train rides back to the deserted playgrounds of their childhood, where couples found themselves forced to repeat the same argument day after day, where young women looked into ordinary mirrors to discover themselves at sixty-five. Each episode brought us into the strange yet familiar place where the distinctions between time, space, imagination, and memory were blurred, where mysteries unfolded and truth was revealed.

We used to play a game, my father and I, in the years before his breakdown. Sitting in the living room with others, he would suddenly say to me with a mischievous smile, "Why don't you go into the bedroom to see if I am there." The possibility always intrigued me. We had played this game before, and I knew that I had no reason to expect to find him: It was impossible for someone to be in two places at once. But I thought there was always a chance, that perhaps this time he really would be there; perhaps he *could* project himself into a second body; perhaps he *could* move through walls while I walked around the long way. Expectant, excited, I traversed the short distance to the bedroom, peered into its blank space. "No," I would say on my return. "No, you weren't there." But sometimes, every now and then, I would be inspired; I would run back to the living room with my wonderful secret. "I saw you," I would tell my father. "I saw you there." And he would nod in perfect agreement.

Heliopolis - Bould: Ismael and Avenue Ibrahim

Top: The rue Ibrahim in Heliopolis, where Felix Zonana grew up, 1920s.
Courtesy of Max Karkegi, L'Egypte d'Antan (www.egyptedantan.com).
Bottom: Nelly Chalom with her sister Céline, Cairo, 1940s.

Felix and Nelly Zonana, Cairo, 1945.

The Chalom family with Rose Zonana in Cairo, 1940s.

Top left: *Nonno*, Selim Chalom, at a Brazilian resort, 1950s. Top right: Nelly and Joyce in Brooklyn in front of Mrs. Rosenblum's house, early 1950s. Bottom: Nelly and Joyce in Brooklyn, 1960s.

Top: Felix Zonana, at his office in New York City, 1960s. Bottom: Joyce Zonana, teaching at the CIGNA Corporation in Philadelphia, early 1980s.

Top: Victor, Nelly, Joyce, and Felix, near Shore Haven, Brooklyn, 1950s.
Bottom: Nelly, Joyce, Felix, and Victor, at Victor's Washington, D.C.,
home, 1995.

Top: Joyce Zonana in her New Orleans garden, 1998. Bottom: Nelly and Joyce in Brooklyn, Grand Army Plaza, 2007. Courtesy of Kathy Asbury.

Six: My Mother's House   ◆ ◆ ◆

If it was my father and I who, again and again, entered the
labyrinth, seeking to find and perhaps conquer the god
within, it was my mother who most often held the thread, tire-
lessly unwinding and then winding it again as we made our
way through the maze's obscure turns. Or if we, thinking we
might cut the cord and find our way alone, got lost, it was she
who retrieved us each time, leading us back with steady resolve.
Neither my father nor I ever attained the labyrinth's dark

Nelly Chalom astride a pony, third from the right, in the desert, early
1940s.

center—the line securing us to the outer world always stopped short. My mother's sturdy pragmatism kept us bound, locked in the everyday, safe from the encounters that might have doomed or redeemed us.

At the same time, she was herself the labyrinth, the unknown space I both feared and desired. My mother's body—strong, vibrant, full, with heavy breasts and long, finely shaped legs—simultaneously attracted and repelled me. While my father was remarkable for his absence, my mother was distinguished by her all-too-palpable presence, thick and redolent of spices, like the heavy *m'ggadereh* and *ful medammes* we ate often, sticky sweet and warm like the aromatic rice pudding and pistachio-studded *ba'alawa* we devoured on special occasions. As a child I was overcome, afraid of her intense physicality, while at the same time inexplicably drawn to her. Because I rarely trusted that the love she offered would not undo me, I fled from her touch, even as I languished for want of care.

During my first few days of life, I could not tolerate her milk, erupting into spasms whenever she tried to nurse me. For several weeks, I lost weight as the doctor sought a formula my body would accept. Even before my birth, locked in the womb, I must have labored against my mother's anxious embrace. I was the first infant she brought to term after a series of devastating miscarriages. The doctor had said it would be impossible for her to have a normal pregnancy. But my mother persisted, taking drugs, praying, determining to have a child. "*Ma'alesh*," the rabbi said, in Arabic, when he learned I was not a boy. "These things happen," the common Arabic phrase implies, "don't feel too bad."

◆

My mother became pregnant with me in October 1948, during the first Arab-Israeli War, which followed the declaration of the state of Israel in May. In June, a bomb killed twenty-two Jews in Cairo's ancient *harat al-yahud*, the poor Jewish quarter. In July, after what was believed to be an Israeli bombing in a residential neighborhood, militant Arabs marched on *harat al-yahud* and set fire to a synagogue. During July and August, four Jewish-owned department stores in Cairo's downtown—a few blocks from the apartment where my mother grew up and where her parents still lived—were bombed and looted. Then, in September, nineteen Jews were killed and forty-two wounded during another attack on *harat al-yahud*. Finally, on November 12, the major Jewish publishing company in Cairo was bombed and destroyed.

All through that year, Egyptian Jews lived under conditions that one observer—perhaps too dramatically—compared to the early days of the Hitler regime. Like the German Jews, the Jews of Egypt must have struggled to determine their identity and allegiance. Were they Egyptians first, inextricably linked to their birthplace, the land where they had prospered and built comfortable lives? Or were they primarily Jews, bound to be loyal to the new Jewish homeland being establishing across the Sinai Peninsula? With whom were they allied in this war? The question could not have been an easy one—for most Egyptian Jews were essentially quietist, not especially observant, not commonly Zionist, and certainly content with their comfortable lives in Cairo and Alexandria.

Whatever any individual Jew might determine for him- or herself, as a group they were suspected by the government and under attack by people in the street. As far as anyone could tell, they might be Zionists; sympathizers with the Israelis; or, worse, active spies and saboteurs. The government sequestered Jewish assets and interned hundreds of Jews. Angry crowds chased and taunted them. Egyptian Jews did not in fact experience the systematic and brutal anti-Semitism of Nazi Germany, but their complacency was shaken.

For nine months in 1948 and 1949, while the streets rang with shouts of "Dirty Jew!" my mother, twenty-seven years old, lay in bed, pregnant with me, immobilized in the apartment she and my father shared with *Nonna*, my father's mother. It was a true confinement. And it was *Nonna* who, some relatives say, had caused the earlier miscarriages by her bad temper and jealous demands; now she brought my mother food she knew my mother didn't like and troubled her with anxiety about her sons. My father's brother Ezra was in the Israeli army, and when my father himself—suspected of having built a bomb in the family kitchen—was arrested and detained, *Nonna* became hysterical. My mother could do nothing: Unable to rise from bed, she had to remain still, listening to her mother-in-law's hysterical cries.

It does not surprise me, then, that I could not drink my mother's milk, steeped as it was in personal and cultural anxiety. Lying in bed alone and afraid, my mother would have had little strength with which to respond to the dangers confronting Egyptian Jews, and even less to defend herself against the ill-will of the mother-in-law who never hid her resentment of her son's beautiful wife.

For my mother *was* a beautiful woman, with thick, wavy black hair and a wide, open smile. Although never slender, she wore clothes that accented her waist and her breasts. Her eyes were dark and distinctive, with dark brown irises, long lashes, and classically arched brows. She allowed herself only two cosmetic adornments: bright red lipstick she applied whenever she left the house and Chanel No. 5 perfume for special occasions. She cut her toenails and fingernails with scissors, washed her hair with Ivory soap. Yet despite her no-nonsense approach to personal grooming, she always exuded a strong sensuality, a raw desire for all that life could offer.

In the old black-and-white photograph I keep in my bedroom, she sits comfortably astride a pale pony, tanned bare legs and arms in sharp contrast to bright white shorts and a V-necked top. Sometimes I imagine that the dark band I see below the white of her blouse is a bare midriff, and perhaps it is; but then I think, no, this is Egypt in the 1940s, that can't be right; it must be a belt. A black scarf frames my mother's hair, and she smiles, her eyes shining. There are nine people in this photo: two women and four men in European clothes, lined up on camels or ponies on the plateau at Giza before the Sphinx and the Great Pyramid, along with two men in long galabias holding the animals and one man sitting cross-legged on the sand. Of them all, my mother is the only one whose smile reveals her teeth, the only one who seems thoroughly at ease in the glare and heat and dust of the desert. The sky in the small, faded photograph is white, shimmering above the ancient stones and parched sand. Acquaintances studying this picture are sure they can find my mother.

"She's the little French woman on the left," they say.

When I point her out—radiant, not so little, in the center, her head beneath the apex of the Great Pyramid—they are shocked.

"She looks like an Arab."

"Yes," I say, "she does."

I am not surprised by my friends' surprise, for I know what they are expecting. They think my mother will look "Jewish," that they will see a clear distinction between Jew and Arab. Yet in this photo, my mother—despite her Western clothes—looks like the native that she is. She inhabits the Egyptian landscape as she inhabits her body—with passion and pleasure. She had been born in Cairo, had grown to adulthood there, had awakened to the world of the senses in its sunlit streets and fragrant gardens. During her childhood and early adolescence, she had taken almost daily walks in the desert beside the pyramids. Why shouldn't she look at home astride a desert pony? Why shouldn't she revel in the sun and sand and heat?

◆

"*Elle avait l'ésprit très large,*" my mother says admiringly of her own mother, when I ask her to talk about what it was like to grow up in Egypt. "She had a great spirit" would be the literal translation, but what my mother means is, "She was very open-minded." My mother's mother, Allegra, allowed her daughter, throughout her girlhood, to take long, unsupervised walks through Cairo. It is a freedom difficult to reconcile with my mother's other recollections of her youth: "We never went out without a chaperone," she says, "we never were out by ourselves." Restrictions must have come during late adolescence, then, and they were imposed not by her mother but by her father. It was her father who thwarted her ambition to attend medical school, enrolling her instead in a course in home economics. And it was her father who chastised her for looking like "*une Arabe*," and who once punished her for laughing in the streets while riding in an open carriage with her brothers. "A decent girl does not laugh with strange men," he had told her. And when she protested that she had been in the company of her brothers, he said it made no difference. "People don't know who they are. You must always act like *une fille de bonne famille*—a girl from a good family."

My mother's *bonne famille* lived in the elegant European center of downtown Cairo, on the fashionable rue Suleiman Pasha (now Talat Harb), a few blocks from the Nile and not far from the massive Adly Street Synagogue, *Char Hashamayim*, "The Gates of Heaven." The Royal Opera House was an easy walk, and Groppi's, the renowned Swiss pastry shop that hosted popular tea dances, was just on the corner. This was the heart of colonial Cairo, the area known as Ismailia, marked by heavy stone buildings with ornate facades lining wide boulevards. Developed in the late nineteenth century by the Khedive Ismail, the neighborhood was designed specifically to attract European investment and to give a cosmopolitan—in fact colonial—air to the North African city. But my mother's walks took her outside this circle of bourgeois European security, into the ancient city of narrow streets and low, worn buildings, where tailored wool suits and leather shoes gave way to loosely draped cotton galabias and bare feet, where donkeys and goats replaced cars and trolleys, and where the dominant language was Arabic, not French or English or Italian.

Most often, my mother went into the desert, to Giza, where the pyramids shadowed the sand. She would cross the Nile and take a tram through the oldest parts of the city, until she reached the vastness of the desert, where she would walk alone for three or four hours in the early morning. None of her friends accompanied her, for there was no one she knew whose parents would allow them this freedom, no one with a similar taste for the solitude and wildness of what was then an undeveloped expanse of desert leading to the huge pharaonic monuments.

"What did you think about?" I ask. "What did you feel?"

"I loved being in the desert," she says simply. "I loved walking alone."

I try to visualize her as a young woman in Egypt, walking with her steady, sure stride across the sand. I imagine her breathing deeply, throwing wide her arms, allowing the rhythm and power of her gait to carry her forward. Alone against the sky, she could feel secure, clear, definite. In the desert, there would be no need to behave like *une fille de bonne famille*, no question of European or native, Arab or Jew, not even male or female—just the elemental vastness. In the desert, my mother could be free. She could expand, filling the sky. I see her as a colossus of that desert, possessed of it.

◆

Marriage, as it did for so many women of her generation, changed her—or at least changed the conditions under which she could live. She tells a story of an afternoon not long after her wedding when she persuaded my father to walk with her around one of the massive garden-enclosed palaces of King Faruq. When they returned after several hours in the hot sun, my father was faint with exhaustion, and *Nonna* severely berated my mother. My mother's days of untrammeled walks were over; her considerable energy turned inward, from public to domestic space, where she now worked assiduously to create an environment that could contain herself and her family. I cannot remember our first apartment in Heliopolis on the outskirts of Cairo, and have only dim memories of our first home in Brooklyn—but the second one, the small two-bedroom apartment in Shore Haven where I lived with *Nonna* and my brother and my mother and father for seven years, remains in my mind as a place of cramped confinement.

There was hardly room to walk, certainly no room to play. In the bedroom I shared with *Nonna* and my young brother, there were two single beds, two dressers, a desk and a crib; in my parents' narrow room there were also two single beds, pushed together at night. In the living room, a sofa bed for our many visiting relatives, a coffee table, several chairs, a large mahogany dresser, a folding mahogany dining table, and a daybed that my brother used when he got older. In the kitchen, a table, four chairs, and cabinets packed with provisions.

Most of our furnishings were hand-me-downs from *Tante* Suze and *Oncle* Joe; but my mother kept everything meticulously clean, waxing the wood, vacuuming the rugs, endlessly dusting, washing, ironing, arranging. A few objects stand out: a small bronze bust of an African woman, with bare breasts tantalizingly displayed; a brass tray engraved with intricate Arabic calligraphy; a watercolor evocation of an ancient Jerusalem street. And always, on every table, the sweet-smelling, brightly colored fresh flowers she craved, flowers my father brought home every Friday night, flowers relatives carried into the apartment when they came for holiday dinners, flowers my mother shamelessly filched from the yards of our unsuspecting Brooklyn neighbors.

Although the apartment was orderly and welcoming to visitors, it was for me unremittingly oppressive: every corner inhabited, every object devoted to a specific place, every closet and drawer carefully organized. I could not lay a book or a cup on a table without having it removed; I could not open a drawer without knowing exactly what I would find. There was nothing hidden, nothing private, nothing I could make exclusively my own. It was not simply that the material presence of my mother was so strong; there was also her powerful will, seeking to mold me into the kind of woman she had herself become: domestic, docile, devoted to family and tradition. I had chores to occupy almost every hour: I too was expected to dust, wash, iron, and vacuum.

Unable to locate myself in my mother's domain, I escaped into books. Reading offered a magical entrance into other lives and other minds, other spaces I might roam at will. Once I discovered books, obtaining my Brooklyn Public Library card at the age of seven, I retreated within their covers at every opportunity—reading in bed, reading sprawled on the couch, reading even under the kitchen table when my mother insisted that I not read while the family ate. My taste tended toward elaborately plotted nineteenth-century novels of romance and adventure: *Jane Eyre* and *Two Years Before the Mast*, *Wuthering Heights* and *Twenty Thousand Leagues Under the Sea*. In the sixth grade I read every novel by Laura Ingalls Wilder, dreaming of little houses on the prairie, in the woods, on the banks of Plum Creek—anywhere but in Brooklyn, in the dull-red-brick apartment buildings of our low-income housing development.

Early on I also developed a rich fantasy world that centered around a secret, private room. The room, which I imagined to be just on the other side of the wall of my real room, was marvelously bare, its only furnishing a small Oriental rug. This was my magic carpet, the vehicle that would transport me to other realms, far from our small Brooklyn home. Alone, I traveled to Paris and London and Tokyo and Rome. All I had to do was sit on the rug, cross my legs, and dream.

For my mother, though, there could be no magical travel. Her world had narrowed, irrevocably, until she could no longer allow herself to think back to her own past—the past before her marriage, the past before leaving Egypt.

"*Je n'ai pas de mémoire*," she tells me when I beg for details about her childhood. "I have no memory."

Conditioned by my years of psychoanalysis, I am reluctant to accept her word. Surely, I tell myself, her lack of memory must be a screen; there must be some trauma or wound she does not want to remember. Of course the trauma, I now see, is the very severing of her early dreams. My mother is adamant. "There is no story," she insists. "There's nothing to say, nothing to know. I have no memory."

Yet sometimes, without being called, the images rise: sensual memories most often, vivid recollections of a scent, a color, the feel of the breeze on a summer night. We might be walking or swimming, and she will say with the shock of sudden recognition: "This, this is what the air was like in Helwan; this is what the light was like in Alexandria; the flowers in the *Jardin Botanique* had this smell." Excited, she tells me about the fruit offered by vendors who called up to her family's second-story balcony: fresh figs, watermelon, pineapples, grapes. My mouth waters as she speaks and I yearn for more; but my mother falls silent again.

One afternoon, we walked together along a North Miami street, the afternoon air hot and thick. My father was close to death in a nursing home nearby. He was there for physical therapy after surgery to repair a broken hip. He was eighty-four and already debilitated by Parkinson's disease, his leg muscles atrophied and his esophagus so rigid that he could no longer swallow. My mother and I had just made the decision not to insert a feeding tube. We were walking now to assuage our grief. Suddenly, my mother's face brightens.

"Look," she points across the street, "look at that mango tree."

We cross to get a closer look, eyeing scores of mangoes, just beginning to ripen, tantalizingly out of reach. Then my mother looks down, sees the fallen mangoes on the ground. We gather dozens, putting them into the large sack she always carries with her.

"I loved the mangoes in Egypt," she says, and a reverie begins.

She recalls the flowers, the scents, the sweetness in the air. "We used to make pickled mangoes," she says, and that night, she fills jars with these Florida mangoes, preserving them with curry powder and vinegar. "I had forgotten how much I loved these." All through the weeks while my father dies, we eat unripe mangoes, the tangy green flesh recalling my mother's youth.

But when I seek stories, when I try to ascertain dates and names and specific events, my mother folds in upon herself, like a flower that opens only for the sun. "I have no memory," she insists. "Even as a girl, I had no memory."

I am reminded of her handwriting: a minuscule scrawl, vague squiggles and loops that barely mark the page.

"Why is your writing so illegible?" I ask, thinking I might find a clue, and for this she has a ready answer.

"I didn't know how to spell when I was in school, so I made my letters all alike, so the teacher wouldn't mark me wrong. I had no head for spelling. Even then, I had no memory."

◆

During the early 1930s my mother attended the small École pour Filles run by Mme Jabbès, an Egyptian Jewish woman who styled herself as a Parisian. It was here that she acquired the rudiments of mathematics and French and English grammar, along with geography, French history, and the tiniest bit of Arabic. My mother recalls her Arabic lessons: "We had a small reader. Whenever we came to the end of the first section, the teacher made us start over. We never got past *'Ahmadou grimpe sur le palmier'*"—a simple sentence early in the primer. Instead of studying the language and history of the country in which they lived, the students at Madame Jabbès's school were steeped in the culture of France, acquiring so much proficiency that when my mother visited Paris at the age of fifty-five, she felt utterly at home. "I knew the streets like the back of my hand. I knew where everything was because we had studied the map in school."

To Mme Jabbès's students, French was the language of high culture, of *"civilisation,"* as my mother still says. And with the knowledge of French came certain notions of propriety. People could be *civilisé* or *pas civilisé, comme il faut* or *pas comme il faut, bien élevé* or *mal élevé, de bonne famille* or *pas de bonne famille*— civilized or uncivilized, proper or improper, well brought up or badly brought up, from a good family or a bad family. These were the categories that separated those who possessed French or European manners from those who lacked them—Jews and Arabs in Egypt, and, once we came to the United States, ourselves and most Americans. For my mother, it was not our Jewishness that set us apart, it was our Frenchness. And it was this sense of French bourgeois decency, inculcated by Mme Jabbès, that sustained her. No matter what our economic circumstances, the table would always be carefully set; clothes, however old, would always be mended, clean, and pressed; and the apartment of course, would be spotlessly clean.

It was at Mme Jabbès's school that my mother met her friend Suze, the woman I still call *Tante,* "Aunt," and who was more to me than any of my mother's sisters—my real aunts, Diane and Céline, in South America. Suze and my mother were in their early teens when they met. It was an immediate, absolute passion, the kind of romantic friendship I myself was to know growing up: You meet someone who is everything you want to be; she sees the same in you and you become as one, sharing secrets, dreaming dreams, becoming co-conspirators in a plot to live more fully than you had imagined possible. During the long Egyptian summers, Suze and my mother went every year with their families to Alexandria or Ras al-Bar, spending several months together by the sea; the rest of the year, Suze spent whatever time she could visiting my mother's bustling downtown apartment. "She was happier with us," my mother tells me. It was in my mother's home that Suze met her future husband, Joe, the brother of *Tante* Céline's husband, Siahou; and it was Joe who in 1948 took Suze and their young son to the United States, where he soon made a fortune as an operator of cargo ships.

Suze was a tall woman, beautiful and elegant, the only one in our extended family with blue eyes and blonde hair—not blonde exactly, but a deep honey color that reflected the sun and amplified the luster of her gleaming gold jewelry. She had long legs and arms, with perfectly manicured oval nails, always lacquered in some creamy peach or pink. When she sat or stood or walked or swam, she seemed always to be utterly poised, utterly comfortable within her burnished, smooth skin. And although I was conscious even as a child that at every moment she was posing, arranging herself for an audience's admiration, she was so thoroughly in command of her art that I was always taken in, dazzled. I was sure she had been born this way—graceful, confident, secure. Try as I might—and for many years, it was all my effort—I could never attain her apparently unselfconscious equanimity. For Suze, with her fair skin and golden hair, her blue green eyes that reflected the sea, was utterly unlike my mother and me: No one would ever mistake her for an Arab, and she blended easily into the elite American world she inhabited. Although she spoke French and served Middle Eastern food (prepared largely by my mother) at her elegant parties, she never appeared to be an immigrant; she bore no trace of the desert wildness that still marked my mother.

I thought of Suze as my godmother, although no one ever identified her that way to me and there are no such things as godmothers in Jewish tradition. I must have grafted onto her whatever I heard about godmothers from my Catholic schoolmates in Brooklyn. Or, more likely, I endowed her with the characteristics of the fairy godmothers I read about in storybooks. To some extent, she cultivated that role, hovering over my life with promises of affection and wealth. *"Tante Suze, çe n'est pas ma vraie tante, m'envoie d'Amerique de l'argent pour acheter un joli bijoux. Une grande partie de ma layette vient aussi d'elle."* (Aunt Suze, she's not my real aunt, is sending me money from

"America," to buy a pretty piece of jewelry. A large part of my layette also comes from her.) I find these words written in black ink in my mother's tiny, nearly illegible handwriting in my lavish baby book, which carries the title *Days to Remember.* The book was a gift from Suze, sent a few months after my birth; the card that came with it, still in its envelope glued to one of the inside pages, reveals that the book was purchased at Saks Fifth Avenue: *"À petite Joyce çe petit livre ou collectioner ses plus charmants souvenirs. Love from Suze."* (To little Joyce, this little book, in which to gather her most charming memories.) After the first few pages documenting my first weeks, the book, alas, is blank.

During the years that I was growing up in Brooklyn, Suze and her family lived in Stamford, Connecticut, on a large estate at the edge of Long Island Sound. Set far back from the road, behind a tall hedge, the house was reached by a curving driveway that showed off wide lawns and flower beds thick with snapdragons and gladioli; along its edges, old oaks and maples extended gnarled arms. The house's formal entrance—a great white door framed by huge white columns—was along this driveway, but the real front of the house was on the other side, facing the Sound. It was there, on a sweeping gray flagstone terrace with a three-tiered fountain at the center, that we usually found Suze and her three boys, sitting at a marble-topped table, just finishing a late breakfast as we arrived, drinking freshly squeezed orange juice from crystal glasses, nibbling pieces of hot *shami* bread, breaking off chunks of tangy *kashkaval* cheese.

If it was summer—and in my memory it was always summer at Stamford—everyone was in bathing suits. Suze had already had her swim. Rushing, my brother and I would take off our shoes and run to the cabana—a gray wooden building at the south end of the beach, with one changing room for men and boys, another for women and girls—where we would tear off our city clothes and pull on our suits. And then, our hearts pounding, we would race to the end of the barnacle-studded jetty, impatient to dive into the warm, salty water.

My mother took us on the long trip to Suze's house—two subways to Grand Central, then the New Haven local to Stamford—at least once a month, getting us excused from school for the day if necessary, and leaving *Nonna* behind in Brooklyn. I wasn't aware of it then—filled as I was with my own excitement—but I see now what great outings these were for her: alone with her children, in the company of her closest friend. Lying on the terrace at Stamford, looking out to sea, my mother might allow herself to remember with pleasure her own childhood summers in Alexandria and Ras al-Bar. At Stamford, as in Alexandria, it was a world of women, a world of muted voices and graceful limbs, of bodies opened to the sun, given over to pleasure.

I remember an afternoon when a group of women had gathered: Vivi and Yoli, Suze's sisters; Diane, my mother's sister, visiting from Brazil; and Stella, my cousin who lived in Colombia. The women were all in bathing suits, stretched on pillowed chaise longues grouped beside the terrace fountain. Earlier in the day they had prepared a mixture of sesame paste and honey in a large white bowl. Now, they spread the thick aromatic paste in narrow strips along their tanned legs. After twenty minutes, each woman grasped a strip of hardened paste near her ankle and pulled up quickly, sharply, grimacing as she did. "Aiii!" The paste peeled away from the leg, bringing with it hair and roots. "Aiii!" the women cried, "aiii!" as each one pulled off another strip.

Then they spread more of the sticky sweet substance, lying a while longer in the sun, then pulling again, screaming, laughing, reaching for more paste. Sometimes one woman helped another to spread the mixture of tahini and honey, pulled the strip off her sister's or cousin's or friend's leg. The women's legs and arms were bright in the sun, gleaming. It was a dreamy, languorous scene, the scents, the sounds, the colors mingling in a reverie of summer. The women rubbed their now-smooth legs with rosewater-scented cream; they lay back in their chairs, sipping from tall glasses filled with iced mango nectar. They spoke in French and Arabic, saying things I could not understand.

Our visits to Stamford were a reprieve for all of us, and my mother's friendship with Suze sustained her. For the rest of her time, she was bound to our Brooklyn home, to the daily effort of caring for my brother, my father, my grandmother, and me. My father was sick, my grandmother querulous, my brother withdrawn, and I wildly rebellious: I wanted no part of her life.

◆

In 2001, my mother moved to New Orleans, to live near me. After my father's death, she had planned to stay in Florida, where she had the beach, some friends, and a comfortable small apartment. Suze was an hour away, my cousin Stella lived across the street, and there was a small community of Egyptian Jews in the neighborhood. But one morning, rushing from her bath to answer the phone, she slipped on the bathroom tiles and broke her hip. For an hour she lay on the floor, after having dragged herself to the phone to call a neighbor. The same doctor who operated on my father performed the needed surgery. My mother recovered and, after a month in rehab, could walk again. I had spent much of that month with her, making sure that the nurses answered her calls, encouraging her to move despite her pain, insisting to the insurance company that her stay in the rehab facility be extended until she could go home alone safely. She had fallen early in December, and I was able to be with her because I was between semesters. But my mother worried about what would happen next time—if she fell again, or was ill, who would help her? She couldn't expect me to be available always.

Uneasily, I made the arrangements for her to move. I was terrified of the change she would bring to my life. After all the years, and despite her infirmity, I was still often overcome by her powerful presence. But I could not imagine leaving her alone in Florida, and she didn't want to move back to New York, where my brother lived. The winters were too cold, and besides, she couldn't count on him the way she could me.

I located a "continuous care community" in Algiers, across the river from the French Quarter, where she could have a small apartment with a patio and a small plot of grass. There was no pool, but she could get to one by bus, and she would be able to walk on the lovely landscaped grounds of the retirement "village." I promised to visit her once a week and we began the process of forging our new, adult relationship. I had just left Kay and was in the midst of setting up a new home for myself; she was struggling to find her footing in yet another new city. Bit by bit, we contrived to meet; I took her to restaurants overlooking Lake Pontchartrain; we searched together through nurseries for the jasmine she remembered from Egypt—"We used to make necklaces of the flowers," she said; I brought her bags of dried hibiscus from the Palestinian grocery so she could make *carcadet*, the bright red brew she remembered from her childhood. We went to the opera, the ballet, even to see my friend Audrey perform *la danse du ventre*—belly dance.

One spring, I took her with me to spend a weekend in a rented house on Dauphin Island, in Alabama—a narrow curving strip of sand bar, frequently battered by hurricanes, with houses built high above the beach. "*Ca me rappele Ras al-Bar*," she said ecstatically when she called Suze in Florida. "It reminds me of Ras al-Bar." For three days, she walked along the shore, played in the waves, sat beside me while I wrote. For too many years, I was caught in my struggle against her, refusing her efforts to make me into a domestic woman. What I wanted, I now see, was something she had had all along—the long desert walks of her Cairo girlhood, the untrammeled freedom of her youth. For years we fought, as she sought to mold me into the *fille bien élevée* she believed it was her duty to raise; but at heart, despite her conscious commitments, she nurtured in me her own dream of independence—her own dream of flight.

Seven: Ocean Avenue ◆ ◆ ◆

When I started having nightly dreams that my mother was cutting my hair, I knew it was time to move out of my parents' Brooklyn home. The year was 1968. I was eighteen, and I had tried leaving twice before—once when I went off to

Tante Suze, Cairo, 1940s.

college just after high school, and a second time, the following year, when I came close to renting a studio apartment on a quiet street in Park Slope. Each of my earlier attempts had ended in failure: the first when I returned from college without completing my freshman year; the second when I allowed my mother to talk me out of making the move. I could do whatever I liked, she promised, if only I would stay home.

But my dreams convinced me otherwise. Each night, I would see my mother approaching me with scissors. She would tie me into a barber's chair, gag and blindfold me, then spin the chair until I was dizzy. I could feel the scissors making sharp, wild cuts, nearly piercing my scalp. When it was over, most of my hair lay scattered across the floor, leaving me with nothing but a few jagged tufts on my head.

It had taken four years to grow that hair. I loved its thick, dark weight, the way it fell over my shoulders and onto my back. Every night, I brushed it faithfully—the requisite one hundred strokes, lulling myself into dreams. I wore it up or down, sometimes half up and half down, twisting strands into what I imagined were artful shapes held in place by elaborate barrettes. Strangers on the subway admired it; boys I knew stroked it. As a child, despite my longing for a ponytail like those of my classmates, I had worn my hair in the short curls my mother favored. But now that I was grown, my hair was mine to do with as I liked. Or so I imagined, until the dreams came.

◆

I kept my plans to myself, locating a cheap, fourth-floor, rent-controlled walkup on Ocean Avenue, not far from Brooklyn College. The building, one of three identical brick structures that lined the street, had a dim central lobby with a worn staircase on either side; on each floor, on each side of the building, four apartments opened out from a small, dark landing. My apartment was at the top right corner of the building, with a bedroom to the east and a living room facing south. I envisioned mornings watching the sun rise over the college clock tower, afternoons drinking tea, and evenings of quiet study looking out into the sky. My part-time job at a veterinary clinic would cover the rent, and I would have few other expenses. I signed a three-year lease—the only choice the landlord offered—and surreptitiously began to move my books and clothes.

◆

"How, Joyce, can you do this to your mother?"

The voice was that of my beautiful *Tante* Suze, calling me a month later, as soon as she had heard the news. For my mother had tried to keep my departure secret. That her only daughter was living in an apartment by herself was *une honte*, a shame, a sign of the family's failure. My father would be mortified if people knew. But Suze, my mother's best friend, must have sensed something was wrong, must have questioned my mother until she confessed.

"You should be out dancing," Suze said to me now in all seriousness. "You should be having the time of your life. You should be finding a husband." Her ordinarily beautiful French-Arabic lilt grew ugly. "You are killing your mother. You know you are killing your mother."

Slumped on my narrow mattress on the floor, I had no words with which to answer this woman I had known since childhood, this beautiful woman I feared and admired and still called "aunt." I could see that she was right; my behavior was killing my mother, or a very large part of her—her dreams for me. Yet I was certain I had no other choice. To have remained at home would have been to court my own death, the devastation of my dreams. For while my family hoped I would marry an Egyptian Jewish man, keeping house for him and raising children who would themselves marry other Egyptian Jews, I cherished another ideal: the life of a writer, an artist, an independent woman—a woman who took lovers perhaps, but never a woman who settled into the domesticity and despair I could see had engulfed my mother. I

125

had read Simone de Beauvoir; I knew that a daughter, however dutiful, owed something to her Self.

But for *une jeune fille*, a young girl, as my mother called me, to live alone, without husband or parents or other relatives, was among the greatest transgressions our Egyptian Jewish immigrant community could imagine. It was, in fact, unimaginable—except in the books that formed my frame of reference and from which I drew my sustenance. No one I knew had done such a thing—even my American friends lived safely either with parents or in school dormitories that in those days still functioned in loco parentis, with strict parietal rules and careful supervision.

On the phone, Suze's assault intensified.

"You should be finding a husband," she said. "You should be out enjoying yourself. Instead you will be in your filthy apartment cleaning your filthy toilet."

We both knew it was not the filthiness of the apartment that was at stake. *I* was the one who was filthy, *I* was the one who would never become clean, no matter how hard I scrubbed. For I was now nothing but an unmarried girl, living alone, living—as all our relatives would understand it—in disgrace. The only explanation for my actions must be that I had given myself up to indiscriminate sexuality, refusing all respectability. I was *une femme perdue*, a lost woman, *abandonée*. I had heard the whispered words before, used to describe someone who had somehow stepped outside the narrow circle of decent society—the world of *comme il faut*. How could I explain? It was not sex that I was after, not really. While still living with my parents, I had contrived to begin making love with a high school boyfriend, and I did not need an apartment of my own to continue doing so. No. In renting those three bare rooms above the Brooklyn trees I was after something else, something I could explain neither to Suze nor to my mother, not even really to myself.

Yet I was indeed, as Suze might have said, *une femme perdue*—adrift in an uncharted and terrifying New World, without bearings or direction. It had taken all my strength to make the move, all my energy to shut the door against my mother's grief and my father's shame. Now that I was in possession of my apartment, what was I to do in it? Most days, I lay on my mattress, unable to rise, afraid to walk outside, paralyzed by the enormity of my offense, overwhelmed by the magnitude of what I had done. Authenticity? A life of freedom and creativity? It was all I could do to brush my teeth each morning and take a shower in the indeed filthy bathroom. The apartment I had imagined as a sunlit aerie loomed now as an alien darkness, inhospitable and cold. Mold grew in the kitchen sink and cockroaches prowled the hall. The empty living room—without furniture or window coverings—echoed loudly to my step. Only in the bedroom, with its mattress on the floor and a few wooden crates stuffed with books and papers, could I find any peace. Yet even there I could not still the voices that told me I was wrong, bad, ungrateful, sick.

"You are killing your mother," Suze said again. "You should be ashamed."

◆

It had been no easier two years earlier when I wrested permission from my parents to attend college away from home. Then I had spent months in loud, tearful fights, invoking the assistance of teachers from my public high school who tried to persuade my parents that it would be good for me to "go away" to school.

"*Ça ne ce fait pas*," my mother had said tonelessly. "It isn't done. Your father will not approve. Girls do not live away from their families. It is *une honte*, a shame, if they do."

But I would not back down. We were in the United States, not Egypt, I shouted, and going away to college was something everyone did. In the end, my parents grudgingly relented. I could go wherever I liked, they said, but I would have to pay my own way.

Encouraged by my teachers, I applied to six colleges, four of them among the Ivy League. When I received my acceptances, I chose Radcliffe—not because it really appealed to me but because I calculated that it would be the most difficult school for me to attend, challenging me socially as much as—if not more than—academically. Not quite seventeen yet, I was awkward and shy, trapped in my sense of foreignness, caught in the narrowness of family and my Brooklyn neighborhood. At Radcliffe I would encounter the fair-haired blue-eyed scions of old American families; I would be forced to relinquish my immigrant ways. I would become, at long last, "American."

On my first day in Cambridge, my roommate, a lanky blonde woman from Wisconsin, told me she had never met a Jew. Never mind that I had never met an Episcopalian. Did I have horns, she asked; could she see them? The other girls in the dorm seemed equally blonde, equally ignorant of the world from which I had emerged. I envied them their straight hair and narrow hips, their pastel mohair sweaters and matching pleated skirts, their easy way of speaking and moving as they gathered in graceful groups for afternoon sherry. Most of them were graduates of private boarding schools; their fathers were lawyers and doctors and U.S. senators; their mothers and grandmothers Radcliffe alums. What did my father do, they wondered, where had I gone to school? It was impossible to say, "My father is a poorly paid bank clerk; my mother is a housewife. I was born in Cairo and grew up sharing a room with my grandmother."

Still, classes at Harvard thrilled me. Each morning I rode my bicycle through tree-lined streets to large lecture halls in ivy-covered stone buildings. The professors spoke of sonnets and revolutions and mitochondria and ions. I took notes assiduously, not wanting to miss a word, reading all my assignments with compulsive care. I was taking History of English Literature, History of Western Civilization, Introduction to Biology, and General Chemistry—the standard freshman classes, each taught by a dynamic and distinguished professor. But the only classes in which I had any personal contact with professors or even other students were the science labs and my two weekly seminars in literature and writing. In the labs I followed instructions and worked silently; in the seminars, I did my best to hide. When my young writing instructor invited me to his office to discuss my work, I could do nothing but cry.

Early in the fall semester, I forced myself to attend a Harvard-MIT freshman mixer. I wore a tight wool knit dress—a rust brown turtleneck—that clung to my hips and breasts. My long hair was twisted into a smooth knot. From my ears hung heavy silver earrings with reddish stones in the center; on my wrists were the gold bangles my grandmother had given me. The large hall at MIT was packed with groups of young men and women, talking loudly, standing uncomfortably, more boys than girls. Knowing no one, I found a spot beside the plates of pretzels and chips. A boy invited me to a slow dance. As we moved stiffly across the floor, he pressed his belly against mine. I could feel his stiff penis, pushing toward me. I was a virgin then, though just barely.

One summer earlier, at sixteen, I had tasted passion while studying biology in a summer program for high school students. Bill, one of our teachers, was a motorcycle-riding Texan who wore cowboy boots and a felt cowboy hat. Returning from a field trip one Saturday, he offered me a ride home on his bike. Afterward, he served me dinner in his small Manhattan apartment. Cross-legged on the floor, we ate by candlelight, listening to jazz, drinking chianti from a raffia-covered bottle. Then, pushing aside the plates, we wrapped ourselves around one another, limbs entwined, open mouths pressing greedily. It became a nightly ritual—candles, dinner, wine, arms, legs. Sometimes Bill's fingers reached beneath my skirt; sometimes mine rested between his thighs. But we never took our clothes off, never went "all the way." I was sixteen and afraid; Bill was twenty-four and aware. At ten each night, we would rise, smooth our clothes, walk awkwardly to the subway station a few blocks away. The train rocked me back to Brooklyn, to my well-made bed in my parents' tidy home.

Now, in Cambridge, there was no house in Brooklyn to return to, no parents' concern for my safety to invoke. I was in precisely the situation my mother had feared. *Une jeune fille de bonne famille*, alone in the world. The MIT boy thrust against me. Could he walk me to my dorm? We made our way through the Cambridge night, buying ice cream cones in Harvard Square, licking them slowly, making them last until we reached my dorm.

My mother had told me that men were animals; she had warned me against their desire. She had never told me about my own, the liquid heat I might feel at my center, the trembling ache at my core. On the steps of the dorm, the boy tried to kiss me. When I turned my face away, he tried again. I ran into the building, closing the door behind me. I heard him promise to call the next day. For the rest of my time in Cambridge, I refused all invitations, answered no calls, spent every night alone in my room or in the library. Days went by without words, without touch. I rode my bike to classes, took notes, ate meals, read my assignments—silent and alone. Most nights, I fell asleep amid piles of books and note cards, pen in hand. Mornings, I found spreading blue ink stains on my sheets and pillows.

◆

In high school, a concerned teacher had counseled me.

"You should talk to a psychiatrist," he said. "You need to talk to a professional."

I had gone to his office, as I did nearly every week, to cry. It was after the summer's romance with Bill. In the fall, Bill had stopped calling. I was convinced that if I had been brave enough to make love, if I could have broken free from my family, I might still be riding behind him on his motorcycle, legs wrapped around his sturdy hips.

"I'm not a professional," Mr. Feldman said gently. "You need to talk to a professional."

But I could not imagine following his advice. I was sure I

wasn't crazy, just sad. Anyone else in my situation would have felt the same way. And besides, I longed to become an artist, an independent woman. Wasn't it the destiny of the artist to suffer? We were reading Kafka and Camus and Dostoevsky in my literature classes. I was watching movies by Kurosawa and Bergman and Godard. Surely I was in good company. Pain was a necessary part of life, I thought, the price of authentic awareness.

Later, at Radcliffe, though, I began to think otherwise. Early in my second semester, a high school friend had what people then called a "nervous breakdown." I went to see her in Brooklyn during spring break and was shaken by what I saw: hair hanging in strings, body covered with sweat, eyes unfocused and afraid. My brilliant and beautiful friend lay in bed emitting strange cries. "The wise take heed," Mr. Feldman said to me when we talked on the phone after my visit, and I didn't need any further exhortations. The next week, back in Cambridge, I made an appointment to see a social worker at the Harvard-Radcliffe Health Center, which, in addition to having medical offices, housed a small infirmary.

"How would you like to stay here for a week?" the man asked after our brief interview.

I was startled.

"I'd like to keep you under observation," he said.

"Sure," I said, "sure," suddenly afraid that he knew something about me that I did not, that my condition must be serious. What did this man think? I hadn't told him the worst— that every day now I imagined knives, swords actually, piercing my abdomen or entering me from between my legs. But clearly he could see my distress.

Five days later three male doctors entered the room where I had lain alone in terror, my solitude interrupted only by visits from nurses drawing blood or by attendants bringing trays of unpalatable food. Was I crazy? Was that why the social worker had wanted me here? For five days I had rarely risen from bed, lying in damp pajamas and trying to read, bewildered by the certainty that I was being chased by a set of grotesque figures: animals, elves, strange twisted beings that exulted in their ability to frighten me. If I had not been crazy before entering the infirmary, surely I was now. Cut off from the stabilizing routine of classes, I slipped into a world of shape-shifting terrors against which I had no defense.

"How are you feeling?" one of the doctors asked, as he settled into a chair at the foot of my bed.

I struggled to find the voice I had not used for several days.

"Fine," I said. "I'm feeling fine."

"Good." The man nodded to the colleagues who stood along the side of the bed. "Yes, you *are* fine. We've arranged for you to see a social worker once a week. The nurse will set up your first appointment. You can go back to your dorm now."

And with another nod, he led the other doctors out of the room.

Fine. I was fine. My atrophied muscles ached; my unwashed hair felt greasy and ugly. Trembling, I rose from the bed and walked to the window, looking down five stories onto the swirling traffic of Brattle Street. Fine. I was fine. The doctor said I was fine. Then why did the traffic look so terrifying? Why was I afraid to step out onto the street? How could I be fine if my body felt like that of a jellyfish or an amoeba, a primitive, transparent being with no strength to resist the pokes and prods of strangers?

I could not imagine returning to my dorm. How would I explain my absence? How would I return to classes? I had missed a week of schoolwork, and I had made no progress in my reading or writing. A research paper on Jean Jacques Rousseau's *The Social Contract* was due the next day. What was I to do?

Panicked, I remembered the social worker. Perhaps I could talk to *him*. He had seemed kindly and concerned. Still in my bedclothes, I searched the building for his office.

"How can I help you?" he asked, when I knocked at his open door.

"I can't go back," I managed to say. "I'm afraid."

"What would you like to do?"

"I don't know."

"What would you really like to do?"

"I want to go home." The words came out unbidden, surprising me. "I want to go home."

"Why don't you?" the man asked.

"I didn't know I could," I said.

"You can do anything you like," he said.

The college would grant me a medical leave of absence. There would be no academic consequences. I could return anytime I chose.

"Yes," I said, "I want to go home."

My mother arrived the next morning. After meeting with the social worker and promising to find a therapist for me in New York, she came to me. Together, we went to the dorm, packed my belongings, and—without saying a word to any of my classmates—took the next plane back to New York. Two weeks later I began therapy with a psychoanalytically trained social worker in Manhattan. And a month after that I knocked at the door of a boy I had known in high school and offered to go to bed with him.

Marty had been a junior when I was a senior; we worked together on the school newspaper and the literary magazine, and he had pursued me with the dreamy passion of a young poet. Convinced from my superficial reading of Freud's *Interpretation of Dreams* that sexual repression was at the root of neurosis, I reasoned that having sex would cure me, freeing me from the restrictions of my family and the isolation that had overcome me in college. Marty lived alone with his mother; she was at work all day, and so we had the apartment to ourselves every afternoon. It was 1967, the Summer of Love, and we gave ourselves over to it with abandon, making love in Central Park, brazenly smoking marijuana on the streets, reading aloud the poetry of Allen Ginsberg and William Blake.

Not wanting to forsake my formal education, I enrolled at
Brooklyn College and began taking night courses. Marty and I
saw each other regularly, but although we were happy together,
I was afraid of what continuing to love him might bring. It
would have been a "good" marriage, for he was Jewish, albeit
not Sephardic, and my parents would have been pleased. But
I did not understand how I could marry—or even live with—
Marty without losing myself, without succumbing to the very
forces that had engulfed my mother. How could I avoid becoming a homemaker, consumed with raising children and keeping
house? Marty wanted a family, an ordinary life. But I doubted
my capacity to hold on to the fragile identity I was just beginning to forge. And while sex with Marty was sweet, it did not
conquer my fears or satisfy my longings: I was still drawn to,
and terrified by, the eyes and hands of the rough men who followed me in the subway and on the streets of New York.

And so, abruptly, without giving any warning, I broke with
Marty, wounding him and unmooring myself. A few months
later, I rented that first apartment on Ocean Avenue. Immediately, I was plunged again into the pain and fear that had
engulfed me in Cambridge. Only now, without the structure
of dorm life to sustain me, I succumbed even more fully to my
internal chaos. It was as if everything I had previously known
fell away. I had to invent life anew: how to make my bed, how
to brush my teeth, how to boil water, how to make a phone call,
how to dress, how to walk, how to laugh, how to sleep. The bare
rooms I lived in opened around me, a blank canvas awaiting my
design. But what life did I want? How could I choose?

Fitfully, I managed to attend classes, and from time to time
I turned in papers when they were due. Men—teachers, classmates, dropouts, and misfits—came across my path and into
my bed. My desire was not so much for passion as for touch:
It was only when I felt another body against mine that I was
certain I shared a common life with the people around me. Sex
became for me a simple proof of my own existence, a ground-

ing of my otherwise dislocated and disordered consciousness. For the sake of that grounding, I submitted to the sometimes tender, more often brutal, embraces of men who rarely sought a second encounter.

Once, a girl I had known slightly in high school sent me a letter. Would I want to see her? Mary Ann was short, with a thin dark mustache.

"She's not your kind," the physical education teacher had told me two years earlier. "Stay away from her."

But Mary Ann had heard about my trouble at Radcliffe. She thought she could help.

The afternoon she came to visit she brought two six-packs of beer.

"You don't mind if I drink?" she said.

We sat on my mattress and she touched my thigh.

"I could love you more than any of those men do," she promised. "I could love you and make you feel good."

I cried while Mary Ann confessed her attraction. I was incapable of love, I told her; I did not deserve her care.

◆

The next summer, someone I had met during my biology summer program three years earlier asked if she might live with me for a few months. She had come back with her boyfriend from college in Oregon and her parents would not let them stay in their house. Would I let them camp in my space? Terry and Neil brought sleeping bags and pillows, filling my living room with their clothes and books and records, infusing the apartment with an unaccustomed sense of normalcy. At night, I tried not to listen while they made love. But during the day, I used their easygoing presence to help me start a project I had dreamed of for awhile: I would paint my three rooms; I would make the apartment mine.

For the bedroom, I chose an inky blue, deep and comforting, like the color of the summer sky an hour after sunset. For the living room and hall, I settled on a light gray, trimmed in pure white. At each end of the hall, the doors would be glossy red. And for the kitchen I planned a creamy salmon, with soft blue vinyl tiles to cover the scuffed linoleum. All through that summer and into the fall, I painted slowly, meticulously, using a brush instead of the roller the man in the paint store recommended.

Before taking on this task, I had only painted one small bookcase in my parents' home; I did not know what the job entailed, but once I began I was happy. Painting, I could focus on the fresh clean color as it was transferred from can to brush to wall; painting, I could escape the turbulent emotions that still whirled through me. There was picture molding in every room of the apartment; and in the living room, wood wainscoting formed a narrow ledge a few feet above the parquet floors. All this woodwork I painted with contrasting semigloss trim: ivory in the bedroom, pure white in the living room and hall. The apartment's many windows, too, had multiple small panes, each framed in wood. I painted all these edges by hand, bringing my face close to the wood, holding the brush tightly, concentrating fiercely, painting just an inch or two at a time. If it took several hours to paint a few feet, I didn't mind; I had little else to do with my time, and when I painted this way I could be fully focused—clear, sharp, bright—as vivid as the line of color that flowed from the tip of my brush.

I lived at 1271 Ocean Avenue for nearly three years. In the end it became the dream home I had envisioned, a finely wrought nest of light and air, a shelter from within which my fledgling self might learn to fly. Finally accepting the reality of my departure, my mother decided not to abandon me after all; she offered to buy me dishes, and we found at a flea market a set of antique hand-painted china, ivory with pink and yellow roses. She gave me her three small Oriental rugs, brought over from Cairo on the boat in 1951; I laid them out ceremonially, sat cross-legged upon them when I wanted to dream. After a year,

I moved my bedroom furniture from my parents' house, and so I had a dresser, a desk, and a proper bookcase within which to keep my notebooks and journals. The living room remained empty, though I covered its walls with multicolored chalk drawings; in the kitchen, I slowly taught myself to make omelets and to create the tabbouleh I had loved since childhood.

Making tabbouleh according to my mother's instructions became a sensual pleasure. I would soak the fine bulgur in a large bowl while I meticulously minced the vegetables: tomatoes, cucumbers, scallions, and great bunches of Italian parsley. After draining the bulgur using a strainer, I would take up handfuls of the grain to squeeze out the very last excess liquid. Then I would use my hands again to toss the bulgur with the vegetables. Fresh lemon juice, olive oil, salt, and an abundance of cumin completed the dish. When the tabbouleh was done, I would gratefully lick my hands, savoring the bits of bulgur and parsley, the tang of lemon, and the warmth of the cumin.

Although I was beginning to learn to take care of myself, my guilt about sex—and my confusion about how to combine intimacy with independence—led to my pursuit of men who hurt me. The worst was a man who had been my philosophy professor—ABD at Harvard and one of the most popular men on campus.

"Relax," he said, when I resisted his desire. "Relax, and let me take you."

It was no use to say that he was hurting me, that the IUD that had been inserted a few months earlier was piercing my uterus and causing me to bleed. Whatever pain I felt must be caused by my resistance. I needed to relax, to open myself fully. He read to me from Norman Mailer ("The Time of Her Time"), cited Henry Miller, and—though we never called it that—raped me night after night.

Because his parents lived not far from my apartment, my professor-lover refused to spend the night with me in Brooklyn; instead, he insisted that I take the subway to be with him in

Manhattan. His apartment, a ground-floor tenement in Hell's Kitchen, was infested with cockroaches and grimy with dirt. Huge metal bars guarded the windows; a "police lock" secured the metal door. Because I was spending all my time with him, I sublet my apartment to a classmate who played loud music and allowed too many friends to visit. The landlord evicted me, and when I went back to gather my things, I discovered that two of my mother's rugs were gone.

I moved into the professor-lover's New York apartment and lived with him for two dark years, typing his dissertation for him, dropping out of college, and taking a secretarial job in publishing. I lost all touch with former friends and refused— like him—to see my family. It was only when I joined a women's consciousness-raising group and haltingly confessed my attraction to another woman that I found the courage to leave.

◆

During the next six years I lived in nine different apartments in and around New York—not counting my time in San Francisco, where I stayed in five different places in the course of eight months. I slept with a few women and with many men, sometimes with couples, sometimes with groups. Most often, during those years, friends who had invited me in soon asked me to leave; I never signed a lease. Once, I retreated to my parents' basement for three months. I was too erratic, people said, too unstable to be trusted. Each time I moved, I carried with me the few accumulating treasures I had come to think of as mine: the one Oriental rug remaining from my mother's cache, the gold bangles and amulets I had inherited from my grandmothers, the brass candlestick I had found somewhere and claimed as my own. No matter how sordid or crowded or ugly the space in which I lived, I'd lay out my rug, put on my jewelry, light a candle to remind myself of who I had been, who I might become. I didn't paint my walls again until fifteen years later, when I bought my little house on the prairie in Oklahoma, where I found myself, against all odds, an assistant professor of English literature at a midwestern university. And then I chose pastel rainbow colors, pink and yellow and lavender and blue, to celebrate my arrival, alone and intact, at the boundary of my dreams.

Eight: All My Relations　◆　◆　◆

At a small Brooklyn dance school, I prepare for the spring recital. I am ten, and this is my first big performance. For three months I have been working to master the routine. Although awkward and self-conscious, I am determined.

Joyce Zonana and Connie Lindemann in Norman, Oklahoma, 1987.

Our group has the opening number. Costumed in black leotards trimmed with a brightly colored fringe, we wear cowboy hats and matching bandannas. As the curtain rises and the music begins, we step into line across the stage.

"O-o-okla-ho-ma!" we sing, "where the wind comes sweeping down the plain."

I've never seen the musical, and I know little about this fabled place of wheat, wind, and rain, but the words and the music take me there. I see hawks, lazy circles, a wide expanse of prairie. With my classmates I exult:

"We know we belong to the land,
And the land we belong to is grand!"

I was sure I had finally arrived when I found myself breezing down the road, a two-lane "straight shot" highway, at sixty miles an hour, listening to Patsy Cline and visualizing myself in new Western boots and jeans. The color-blocked landscape—brazen red dirt, yellow gold fields, indigo blue sky (like an infinitely stretched, frameless Mark Rothko canvas)—branded my flesh, searing me with an intensity I could not have foreseen. In the distance, tall windmills spun tight circles against the horizon. At the café where I stopped, I drank iced tea from a quart-sized Mason jar and ordered chicken-fried steak. This, I told myself, was "America," the open land of opportunity and freedom I had read and dreamed about, and here I was, at its center. Exhilarated, I embraced the drama of my new identity.

Nine months earlier I had lain sobbing on the floor of my apartment in Philadelphia, where I was then living, immobilized with my first and only migraine after failing my driver's test for the second time. At the age of thirty-seven, I was sure I would never acquire this most rudimentary of American skills. For years I had refused every opportunity to learn, clinging to my status as an urbanite committed to public transportation.

But now driving was a necessary adaptation to the new territory I was about to enter. I had accepted a teaching job in Oklahoma, and I knew that my subway-riding days were at an end. After five perfunctory lessons from the Sears Driving School, I was pronounced ready to take the test. And though I was not surprised when I failed the first time, I had hoped to pass on my second attempt.

From the moment he entered the car that I had borrowed from a friend, the white state trooper unnerved me. Faced with his unsmiling equanimity, I grew clumsy and confused. When he said, "Left," I turned right; when he said, "Stop," I accelerated. In this stolid man's unblinking presence, as in the presence of all those I imagined to be the custodians of "America," I felt my body thicken and grow dark. My hair seemed suddenly coarse and unruly, my shorts ill-fitting and inappropriate. Perhaps I should have worn a dress, I told myself—stockings, heels, makeup. Sitting beside the trooper, I became conscious of the excesses of my female body— overfull breasts, hips, thighs; I could feel and smell the sweat collecting under my arms and between my legs. My fragile competence—as a driver, or as anything else—vanished. Tongue-tied and ashamed, I barely nodded when he told me I had failed.

Driving me home after my ordeal, my friend tried to console me. "You'll do fine next time," he promised. But I could not be comforted. I was sure there would be no next time, that I would be forever stymied, held back by a proliferating phalanx of state troopers, neatly arrayed in dull uniforms, communicating to one another with silent nods. Helpless before them, I knew I was grounded, confined forever to the East Coast, unable to master the rules of the road.

◆

"Do they know about Jews there?" my father had asked when I announced the offer of a tenure-track job at the University of Oklahoma. For the previous five years, I had been apply-

ing for teaching positions, diligently forwarding my credentials
to whatever college or university advertised an opening in my
field. I paid little attention to where the schools might be: California, Wisconsin, Wyoming, Texas—each seemed equally distant, equally unlikely. In the end, Oklahoma was the only offer
I received.

"Aren't you afraid?" my father persisted. "We know nothing
about that part of the country."

"Yes, of course, I'm afraid," I longed to confess. "I'm terrified."

But the imperative to implement my plans kept me silent. I
had to maintain my courage, pretend that this was nothing more
than another easy step in the inevitable process of fulfilling my
dream. I had just completed a Ph.D. in English literature at an
Ivy League university; what had I been doing for the past nine
years if not working to earn a position as an assistant professor?
Jobs were hard to come by, and my adviser assured me this was
a "good" one. Looking around at my unemployed classmates,
many of whom would be taking nonacademic positions, I knew
I should be grateful. But in my heart, I was chilled.

Oklahoma. I envisioned a barren, flat landscape, unbroken
by anything except oil wells. I imagined an entire state populated by Protestant fundamentalists, fair-haired and fair-skinned
descendants of the pioneers, who would inspect me with the
bland indifference, if not contempt, of the state trooper. To
move to Oklahoma from the multicultural security of my East
Coast niche seemed like nothing less than stepping off the edge
of the world. Yet, despite my terror, I knew I could not refuse
to go.

It was not simply that I was being offered the rare chance
of a "good" job at a "good" school; much more significant was
the fact that Oklahoma represented for me the ultimate challenge, the challenge of "America." Although I had lived by then
in the United States for more than thirty-five years, I had never
been able to shake the sense of being indelibly "other," incurably

alien. I had no memories of Egypt, no real sense of having lived there as an infant. I had mastered the English language and even earned a Ph.D. But I still thought of myself as just off the boat. Neither college nor graduate school, neither friendships nor love affairs, had succeeded in eradicating my difference.

On the New York subway, dark-skinned strangers still spoke to me in foreign tongues: Arabic, Spanish, Greek, Hindi. Instinctively, other immigrants knew I belonged among them, even if they couldn't identify my tribe. Walking through New York and the ethnic, working-class neighborhoods of Philadelphia, I felt at home. Dark skin, dark eyes, lilting accents and the rich exuberance of Mediterranean and African and Caribbean people put me at ease. It was blonde paleness that disconcerted me, the veneer of patrician politeness that made me lose my composure. I struggled to contain myself as a proper American, trying to act *comme il faut* as my mother might have put it, but I never could: some unruly emotion, some untamed flesh, some unspoken desire always betrayed me.

When I was introduced to new acquaintances, I steeled myself for the inevitable question.

"Zonana," people would muse. "What kind of a name is that?"

When I would respond, "Egyptian Jewish," their wonder would grow.

"I've never met an Egyptian Jew before," they would say.

Indeed, I could have told them. I was exotic, one of a kind—an undissolved, indigestible grain in the otherwise tasty blend of "America." No matter how far I traveled from my family's visions of me as a dutiful Egyptian Jewish daughter—accumulating lovers, jobs, degrees, friends—I still could not integrate myself into the American mainstream. No matter what I did, I remained to myself an anomaly, a strange amalgam of ancient custom and contemporary ambition.

So, as I clutched my English Ph.D., it became imperative that I go to Oklahoma, if only to test myself against "America," to discover whether I could really live in this country of which I had been a citizen for so long. As I had done twenty years earlier when I went off to college, I decided to move to the one place that frightened me the most.

My New York friends stared in disbelief.

"Omaha?" they asked. "What will you do in Omaha?"

"Oklahoma," I replied, trying to stay calm. "Oklahoma. I'm moving to Oklahoma for a teaching job. I went to graduate school so I could get a teaching job."

"Idaho? Why would you want to move to Idaho?"

"Ok-la-ho-ma," I'd say again, but few New Yorkers could keep the indigenous American syllables straight. "Red People," I should have said, but I didn't know that yet. The Sooner State. Indian Territory. The last frontier.

◆

I didn't start graduate school until I was in my late twenties, for I hadn't completed my undergraduate degree until then. After leaving college in my freshman year, I had gone to school only fitfully, taking classes for a semester or two, then dropping out again. It was too hard to maintain my focus. For several years, I worked as a secretary, and then as a copywriter, for paperback publishing companies in New York. I took whatever work I could get, lived wherever I could find a place. The sudden death of an older friend startled me into an awareness of finitude: I knew all at once I needed to choose, to make a plan for myself and stick to it. I would become a teacher, I determined, a teacher of writing. Within a year I had completed my undergraduate degree and in the fall of 1976 I entered the English Ph.D. program at the University of Pennsylvania in Philadelphia.

I took easily to life in West Philly's comfortably decaying streets, experiencing the campus, and especially the library, as a sweet haven, a calm and welcoming sanctuary after my confused wanderings of the previous decade. A fellowship enabled me to spend my days reading and, after a few years, teaching the literature I loved. New York was less than two hours away by train, and I could see my old friends even as I made new ones. The transition was easy; I had the clarity of a fresh start without the trauma of a break. Grateful to have made a commitment to something at last, and eager to make up for lost time, I threw myself into my studies with passion and pleasure. The years went by quickly; I put off writing my dissertation as long as possible, but by 1985 I had completed the degree and was ready for what my professors called a "real" job— tenure track, competitive, in a place you would never think of going to otherwise.

I moved alone, accompanied only by two cats, and shipping a small truckload of possessions: books and bookcases, a dining-room table salvaged from Mrs. Rosenblum's Brooklyn house, the old sofa bed that had occupied my parents' living room, a new wooden desk my brother bought me to celebrate my completion of the Ph.D. degree.

When I stepped off the plane at the Will Rogers Airport in Oklahoma City, I burst into tears, unable to compose myself despite the fact that I was being met by one of my new colleagues. That first night, in a low-ceilinged apartment in a faculty-student housing complex on the edge of town, I spread my sleeping bag on the carpeted floor and watched a full moon rise over the prairie. As my cats explored the empty rooms, I tried to imagine how I could live in this new landscape. I felt as if I had crossed, not the Mississippi, but the Atlantic, or some other immense, unknown body of land or water—that I had moved, not to a new city or state, but to a new country, an entirely new territory where language, customs, and topography were entirely unknown. I could see no continuity between this world and the one I had left behind.

Was this how my parents had felt when they moved to the United States? Separated from family, friends, familiar objects and places; scents, sounds, customs and tastes? Alone, with no support or guidance? Was this a reprise of *their* dislocation? No matter how hard I tried to remind myself that I had chosen to come here, that this was a positive move, made for the sake of my "career," I was overwhelmed by the conviction that I had in fact been exiled, unwillingly expelled from one life and cast into another. It was a familiar feeling; whenever I moved I experienced the same confusion: Had I chosen to leave, or had I been forced? Was I moving freely toward something I wanted or was I being denied something I loved? It was as if, again and again, I enacted the drama of my parents' departure. Yes, they chose to leave Egypt. But no, they didn't do so freely. Not exactly. My move to Oklahoma felt the same. And I was even more alone than my parents had been when they arrived in New York: I had absolutely no relatives or acquaintances in this strange new land. They at least had had each other.

In the hardware store on Main Street, the quiet man in jeans and a plaid shirt said, "Sure don't," with a gently rising lilt to his voice when I asked if he carried batteries in the shop. I struggled to interpret his reply, the bland geniality of "sure" clashing against the plain denial of "don't." "Sure don't," the people around here said with broad smiles and flat accents, "sure don't." The words were English, I knew that, but the meanings eluded me. "Are you all right?" a concerned police officer asked one afternoon as I walked alone to campus from my apartment. No one walked on the sidewalk-less streets of this town, and in those first months, before I acquired a car, I stood out wherever I went—exposed and vulnerable, starkly outlined against the bright blue, endless sky.

At the university, I was one of a handful of Jews, and the only lesbian willing to declare herself one. I taught my classes and managed to get through dinner parties and department meetings, but try as I might, I did not know how to place myself. When I went back east for brief visits, I felt it impossible to communicate my despair. It took all my strength to return to Oklahoma after those visits; when I changed planes in St. Louis, I watched with dismay as dark skin and brightly colored clothes gave way to pale faces, big hair, and ten-gallon cowboy hats.

Then, in the spring of my first year, I took the step that marked the beginning of the end of my exile.

"This is the only neighborhood I like in Norman," I said to a colleague who was driving me to meet a friend. "This is where I would buy a house if I were going to buy a one." I thought I was just speaking hypothetically; I had never consciously planned to buy a house.

But it turned out that the woman to whom I was being introduced had just put her house on the market. A vibrant and outspoken professor of social work and women's studies, Connie was retiring after more than twenty years at the university. The daughter of Russian immigrants, she had grown up in the Bronx, and her New York accent was still thick, undiminished by her years in Norman. Her little house, a three-bedroom brick ranch with attached garage and a huge yard, was perfect: small, manageable, well cared for, and very inexpensive. If Connie had managed to make herself a home on the prairie, perhaps I could too. I couldn't think of a good reason not to buy it. We struck a deal, and I moved in just before the start of the fall semester of my second year.

The first week, I pried up the wall-to-wall shag carpeting that blanketed all the rooms except the kitchen, uncovering a pristine oak floor. From a local lumberyard, I bought dozens of feet of quarter-round oak molding that I painstakingly sanded and varnished, then had cut and nailed into place. At the paint store, I pored over colors, bringing home chips that I taped to the walls, examining them under different light. Over the next few months I painted every wall in every room: soft pink to match the built-in 1950s electric range in the kitchen, pale yellow in the living room, periwinkle for my bedroom, peach for the study and guestroom. Shopping for the first time at Sears, I ordered custom-fit metal miniblinds for all the windows, and installed them myself. In the kitchen, I replaced knobs on all the cabinets and hung vertical blinds over the sliding glass doors that opened onto the yard. And in the yard, along my more than fifty feet of fence, I planted hundreds of red and yellow tulip bulbs.

My work on the house and yard was relentless, obsessive. I dreamed about and planned and contemplated each choice of color and fabric and texture, working to create a home that would match my inner vision. I knew that without such a home, my spirit would wander, seeking to return east. While colleagues wrote books and lectures, I painted and sanded and planted. Succumbing to the romance of suburban domesticity, I bought a used lawnmower and pushed it each week across my huge lawn; at Sears I found a wooden picnic table, which I placed beside the barbecue grill just outside the kitchen door. Every day, I parked my new car in the attached garage, using my automatic garage door opener to open and close the entrance. Bit by bit, I learned how to live in Oklahoma.

When Christmas came the next year, I was ready. I would have my first tree. As a child, I had always wanted to celebrate Christmas, imagining that if only we had a tree, we might be truly American. My parents refused: We could enjoy Christmas but at a distance. They would drive us through Italian neighborhoods in Brooklyn to see the decorations, and we would go into Manhattan to admire the tree at Rockefeller Center, but we could not have a tree of our own. We were *Jewish*, my mother reminded me, *Egyptian*: Such things were not for us. But far from my family and living in Oklahoma, what was to stop me?

I selected a small balsam fir and made a guest list for the tree-trimming party I was determined to have. I handwrote invitations on white construction paper, coloring them with bright crayons. Poring through a stack of cookbooks, I selected cookies with exotic German names—*Pfeffernüsse* and *Pfaffenhütchen* and *Lebkuchen*—and assembled the ingredients: allspice and ginger and honey and nuts, citron and nutmeg and cinnamon. As guests arrived, the house was warm with the aroma of mulled cider and eggnog, mingled with the sweet scent of fir. I was giddy with delight. Here I was in my own house in Oklahoma, hosting a

Christmas party, with homemade cookies, hot spiced drinks and a tree of my own in the corner of my living room. People had brought beautiful ornaments—blown-glass heirlooms, antique painted wood, contemporary curiosities crafted from glitter and felt. I hung each one upon the tree. There were angels and trumpets and butterflies and fish, globes and bells and fairies and snowflakes. One of my students brought a beautiful leaded-glass star, with a pansy pressed into its center. The star was six pointed, a Star of David.

Perhaps it was that star, or a lull in the conversation, or one too many repetitions of my tape of "Silent Night." I suddenly knew that something was very, very wrong. Who were all these people walking around in my house? What were they doing, gathered around a Christmas tree? A Christmas tree? What was *I* doing? What was *I* thinking? What had *I* been trying to prove? I suddenly saw myself, an Egyptian Jewish immigrant, playacting at being American, alone in the very middle of the United States, far from anything I could truly call home. Who was I trying to fool? When the guests finally left, I promised myself I would never do anything like that again. The next year, I invited a handful of people to join me in lighting a menorah and feasting on latkes at Hanukkah; in the spring, I conducted a seder, using a women's Hagaddah that focused on the universal themes of bondage and freedom, exile and homecoming.

◆

Although I did not realize it when I moved there, I already knew more about Oklahoma than I thought. In the fifth and sixth grades, I had read all the Little House novels of Laura Ingalls Wilder. My favorite had been *Little House on the Prairie*, the lovingly rendered account of the Ingalls's homesteading experience in Indian Territory. Filled with sensuous evocations of the land, the book seduced me with its unabashed romance of the West, giving shape to my childhood fantasies of escape from the confinement of our family home. So when I bought my house in Norman, I merrily called it my "Little House on the Prairie," not realizing that the Ingalls had in fact lived in the Sooner State; I always pictured them in Kansas, the land made familiar by *The Wizard of Oz*.

But when I reread *The Little House on the Prairie* in Norman, with a firmer grasp of the geography and history of the central part of the United States, I saw clearly that what Wilder calls "Indian country," the red-dirt land south of the Canadian River, was in fact what would later become Oklahoma—Indian Territory, set aside for the Five Civilized Tribes after their forced removal from the Southeast. The Ingalls were illegal settlers in an area that had not yet been opened to white homesteading.

"Pa had word from a man in Washington that the Indian Territory would be open to settlement soon," Laura's mother tells her, making it clear that the Ingalls were gambling on the promise of the Dawes Commission, established in 1893 with the intention of persuading Indians to leave the land they had been granted some forty years earlier.

"The only good Indian is a dead Indian," blusters one of the Ingalls's neighbors, but Pa has a different opinion, and he tries to teach his children respect for the natives. At one point, Laura considers the implications of her family's decision to live in Indian Territory.

"Will the government make these Indians go west?" she asks when a group of hungry Indians camp near their homestead.

Pa says yes, and explains: "When white settlers come into a country, the Indians have to move on. The government is going to move these Indians farther west, any time now. That's why we're here, Laura. White people are going to settle all this country, and we get the best land because we get here first and take our pick. Now do you understand?"

Laura remains troubled. "But, Pa, I thought this was Indian Territory. Won't it make the Indians mad to have to—"

Pa cuts Laura off, tells her to sleep.

Interestingly enough, *Little House on the Prairie* ends not

with the further removal of the Indians but with the displacement of the Ingalls family. In this case, the U.S. government—
in the face of uprisings by the Osage—decides to keep its promise to the Indians just a little longer, and it is the Ingalls who
must move on.

◆

Oklahoma, I discovered not long after I arrived there, is indeed
Indian territory, a state with one of the largest Indian populations in the United States, a place where the native presence is
palpable, permeating the open landscape. There are no reserva-
tions in Oklahoma—the entire state having once been a reservation—and Indians live throughout the countryside. Even
as I engaged in my suburban romance, the presence of Native
Americans also drew me, pulling me into deep awareness of
the land and its inhabitants. Growing up on the East Coast, I
had only the most rudimentary knowledge of native life; I had
not progressed much beyond the stereotypes of film and television. I had loved Princess Summer-Fall-Winter-Spring on *The
Howdy Doody Show*, been impressed by the laconic wisdom of
Tonto, remembered some vague lessons about Pocahontas and
Sacagawea in grammar school. But had I ever thought about
the lives of Indians? Had I ever tried to imagine their culture,
their history, their experience of European conquest? Hardly.
In Oklahoma, these questions—and some of their answers—
became inescapable.

Early on, a native colleague invited me to an intertribal
powwow, deep in the prairie north of Oklahoma City. Awed
to silence beneath a huge sky, I watched as Kiowa, Coman-
che, and Apache men and women drummed and danced far
into the night. Not long afterward, another colleague suggested
we drive the ninety miles southwest toward Lawton, into the
Wichita Mountains Wildlife Refuge. It was his favorite place,
he said, and he thought I might like it too. The Wichitas, an
ancient range of worn granite and limestone mountains, rise

153

abruptly from a huge expanse of open land—"islands in a prairie sea," as the brochure from the National Park Service calls them. Held sacred by the Kiowa, the mountains were considered by the Plains Indians to be the center of the world, the home of the Great Spirit, a place of vision and ceremony—not unlike Delphi for the ancient Greeks.

We drove to the top of Mount Scott and looked out over the wide land. Above the waving grass of the prairie, rocky hills rose, covered with granite boulders of gray and red; between the boulders grew small dark oaks and pale green sage. Eagles sailed above us, and in the distance I could see a herd of grazing buffalo. Drawn to their enduring calm, I found myself returning to the Wichitas again and again. During the four years I spent in Oklahoma, those mountains became my refuge, a place where I could dream, letting myself roam. Most often, my reveries took me to contemplation of native history, to empathy for the displaced and devastated tribes and the deliberately slaughtered buffalo. Once, atop Elk Mountain, I encountered a lone buffalo bull that had climbed the mountain to die. Watching the eagles circling above, I gathered sage to burn in my prairie home.

On the surface, then, I tended my suburban house and managed to hold my "good" academic job. I adapted to mid-America and learned to accept its cool embrace. But the real drama of my life lay elsewhere, in my unexpected awakening to the abiding beauty and power of the land and to the lives of its indigenous peoples. It was in Oklahoma, surrounded by the spirits and touched by the lives of contemporary Native Americans, that I discovered the kind of American I wanted to be: one with respect for ancestors, responsibility for future generations, and love for the land upon which I walked.

◆

When I left Oklahoma in 1990 to accept a teaching position in New Orleans, it was wrenching to say good-bye to the red land and my little house upon it. Once again the choice had been mine: I was eager to work in an urban university, and my partner, Ruth, wanted to start law school. But once again, no sooner had I made my decision than I felt that I was being forcibly ejected from a place I had loved. And I became certain that I could never love and belong to another place again. I cried for the entire 850 miles of our drive south to New Orleans, and I cried every night during our first six months in the city. Ruth left me and I had to find my way on my own again. I bought another little house, tried to make friends, and threw myself into my work. Nothing served me, until one day an acquaintance invited me to a "moon lodge" on the country property of her friends Mary Ann and Medicine Hawk. I had no idea what a moon lodge might be, but I agreed to go along.

Late on a hot July afternoon, after a morning of heavy rains, we drove across Lake Pontchartrain to the sandy terrain of tall pines and winding rivers of the North Shore—markedly different from the low-lying swamp that is New Orleans. We arrived at dusk, just as the full moon was rising. I saw a small house, tall trees, a tepee, and a low round hut, fashioned from canvas cloths covering a bent willow frame—the lodge. Already a group of women were gathered, building a fire. My friend and I joined them. First we laid down a square base of logs, then placed more than two dozen large rocks upon it. Around the rocks, we arranged more logs to form a densely packed cone, leaving openings to the east and west, so that air might circulate; we then pushed straw—the kindling for the fire—into those openings.

We gathered in a circle to light the fire; once the blaze had begun, Medicine Hawk, barefoot and bare-chested, his dark hair pulled back in a long ponytail at the nape of his neck, came forward to tend it. The rest of us walked deeper into the woods to a circle of stones, where we would perform a small ceremony. As we walked away, single file past a meadow, I kept looking back at the huge fire, watching Medicine Hawk's silhouette moving against the flames. The sight burned itself into my memory, an image that seemed to arise in another place and time, archetypal, ancient: man and fire.

For the next several hours, as the fire burned down and the rocks heated, the women sang, danced, and talked. Then we gathered in the teepee, where Medicine Hawk's wife, Mary Ann, led us in a pipe ceremony, and one woman read the story of White Buffalo Calf Woman, the sacred woman who was said to have brought the pipe to the Oglala Sioux.

It was time for the lodge. The rocks were glowing red, and we would be going into the small hut I had noticed when we first arrived.

"The lodge is the womb of the Earth Mother," I was told. "The rocks are Her bones."

I removed my jewelry and took off my clothes, wrapping myself in a cotton sarong that one of the women offered me. On hands and knees, I prepared to crawl in.

"There's nothing to fear but your Self," Medicine Hawk assured me when I hesitated.

Hardly comforted, I nevertheless made my way in, smelling the straw that covered the damp, rich earth. It was dark and round in the lodge, dark and round and damp. I found a place beside the door, hugged my knees to my chest, and waited. Once all the women were inside, Medicine Hawk began to bring the rocks in. At the center of the lodge a pit had been dug into the earth. Each rock was placed here, then sprinkled with a mixture of aromatic herbs: sweetgrass and cedar and sage and tobacco.

The door flap was closed, and the dark surrounded us. I breathed in the sweet scent of the herbs, let the heat warm me. The women were all silent, until Mary Ann began to invoke the four directions: East, South, West, and North. She called on the spirits of each direction in turn, naming Eagle, Coyote, Bear, and Wolf; air, fire, water, and earth; dawn, noon, sunset, and night: the energy of new beginnings, the blossoming of growth, the ripeness of maturity, the fulfillment of age. The simplicity and completeness of the ceremony held me. She called to Father

Sky and Mother Earth, the Grandmothers and the Grandfathers. All the world was gathered here in the lodge, and I was held here as well, embraced by the darkness.

There were four rounds to the lodge, four times when stones were brought in, four times when prayers were repeated. During the third round each woman prayed silently or aloud, ending her meditations with the statement "All My Relations." I joined my voice to those I heard around me, praying for myself, for my family, for my grandmothers and the grandfathers. Over the next nine months, I attended the lodge at each full moon, giving myself over to the rhythm that marked the sky. I listened to Medicine Hawk and to Mary Ann, following their instructions, watching their ways. Each month, I voiced my prayers for healing, and each month I repeated the simple words, "All My Relations." Slowly, I came more and more into my own body, came more and more into my Self. It began not to matter where I lived, in Louisiana or Oklahoma or New York or Cairo. I saw that my one true home was Earth, and that my allegiance belonged to Her.

Nine: Ahlan Wa Sahlan   ♦   ♦   ♦

"I don't understand why you want to go," my mother complained. "There's nothing there for us anymore. *C'est tout perdu. C'est tout finit.*" We'd had this discussion many times before, and neither one of us could think of anything new to say. I wanted to visit Cairo, she didn't see the point.

Inside the Rambam Synagogue. Courtesy of Yves Fedida, Association Nebi Daniel (www.nebidaniel.org).

My father, lost in the dementia that accompanied his advanced Parkinson's disease, was silent. Because I knew that he was close to death, I was making my plans with a new urgency. I wanted to go while he was still alive, so that we might talk about whatever it was I found. For although often he was not with us in the present, his memories of the past were sharp; he talked with clarity and precision about his early days in Egypt.

"You'll hate it," *Oncle* Siahou promised. He was the only one among us with any current knowledge of the place. Close to eighty and in ill health, he still managed to go back several times a year, trying to settle a lingering property dispute. "The city is filthy and crowded—nothing like it used to be."

"Where will you eat?" my cousin Stella, Siahou's daughter, asked. "Where will you stay?" She had accompanied her father a few years ago and had no desire to go again. She assured me that the only decent places were the Nile Hilton or the Semiramis Intercontinental.

But I had made inquiries and identified a hotel I thought would suit my own, very different needs. The entry in *The Lonely Planet* promised "a great deal of colonial charm" in a building that was once the British Officer's Club and, before that, the private bathhouse of the Ottoman Turkish leaders. Although "deteriorated," the Windsor was centrally located, clean, safe, and cheap. I could have a room with a bath for less than forty dollars a night, breakfast included. "One of the only hotels that still feels like Cairo as it used to be," reported another guidebook. Just what I was looking for—not a return to the colonial past, but a glimpse of the lives my parents might have known in the 1930s and 1940s, before the nationalist revolution that transformed the city. I checked with a colleague who knew Cairo well. She had never stayed there herself, but many of her friends had, and she had been to the Windsor for drinks, taking the manually operated wire-cage lift up to the second-floor lounge. "I think you'll like it. And it's very close to Talat Harb, the street that used to be Suleiman Pasha," the street that my mother had grown up on in the elegant downtown neighborhood of Ismailia, after Khedive Ismail, who ruled Egypt from 1863 to 1879, developing a Cairo to rival the great cities of Europe. I sent a fax to the number in the guidebook and received a prompt reply. For an extra five dollars, someone would meet me at the airport.

◆

After nearly three decades of deliberation, I am at last on my way to Cairo—a pilgrimage my relatives do not hesitate to call foolish, but that I know to be essential. Several times already, I have come close: I've contacted travel agents, learned the price of a ticket, toyed with possible dates. But then I would hear about a bombing, a hijacking, a fatal attack on tourists visiting an ancient site, and my resolve would crumble. "It's not safe," I would tell myself, "I won't be able to manage there alone." I am, after all, female, Jewish, and American—all characteristics, I believed, that would make me vulnerable in Egypt. I would be a target, an easy mark. Men would accost me on the street and follow me to my hotel; shopkeepers would suspect that I was Jewish and refuse to serve me; at the airport when I was ready to leave, officials would examine my passport, discover my nationality, and detain me. It was impossible to think rationally about what ought to have been a simple journey back to my birthplace. My family's reluctance to reopen the door they had closed nearly fifty years ago made my own desire seem the most daring transgression. Surely I would be punished for my temerity: the terrorist who brought down my plane would be answering a call, if not from God, then from my own unconscious.

In the weeks before my departure, I pile my desk with maps and brochures. I read books about ancient and modern Cairo, consult with colleagues who have lived in the city, try to learn as much as I can. But still, Cairo as a contemporary city fails to come into focus. It remains for me a place of the past, locked within my parent's unvoiced memories—invisible and intangible, and ultimately inaccessible. Will I find *that* place? Or will I too turn, bewildered, from the dusty modern city, bemoaning the loss of what can never be retrieved—the colonial ease that drenched their childhood in a golden light? The pyramids and the pharaohs hold no charm for me; I have no interest in mummies or ancient tombs; what I seek is some tangible experience of the world in which my parents lived as well as an encounter with the world that has replaced it. I want to meet late twentieth-century Egyptians—including the members of the Jewish community who remained behind after the transformations of the 1950s and 1960s.

At night, I have confused dreams about missed connections and serendipitous encounters. In one, my mother and I, after a bitter disagreement, take different roads to a place where a beautiful young woman serves us tea; in another, I discover in a crowded antique shop a perfectly sculpted statue of a woman's head, and I know that it is mine. During the day, I busy myself painting the bathroom and hall of my New Orleans home. I've chosen a deep rose pink and a dark moss green. Only a few days remain before my trip, and I am twisting myself into absurd corners, bending backward at the top of the ladder to reach the strip of wall above the bathtub tile. It takes three coats of paint to cover the bathroom, and I work assiduously. Sometimes lying on my back, sometimes squeezing myself between the sink and the tub, I apply the paint with a narrow brush, absorbed in the process of transforming this tiny space. I remember what a friend told me when I first moved here: New Orleans is at the same latitude as Cairo; like Cairo, it crowns the delta of its continent's longest river.

◆

On the plane—TWA flight 888 to Cairo and Riyadh from JFK, New Year's Day, 1999—a large, fair-skinned American man in the seat in front of me takes umbrage at a short, dark-skinned Egyptian who is jamming his bag into an overhead compartment. "That's *my* jacket you're crumpling," the American complains loudly. "If you had gotten here on time you wouldn't have this problem." He says something to his wife, about how *they* always do this, and I wince. The Egyptian says nothing. I have been in my window seat for a while now, trying to convince myself that I am actually on a plane to Cairo. For all I can tell at first, I could be going to London or Madrid or even Texas. The plane is filled with businessmen as well as some young people with heavy backpacks. But now women in tight headscarves begin to come on; they carry packages tied with string and search anxiously for their seats. I hear voices speaking in Arabic. One flight attendant wears dozens of silver bracelets on her arm; "I got them at the Khan al-Khalili—the old market in Cairo," she tells me confidentially when I compliment her. The last person to board is an old woman, nearly blind. She is led to her seat by a young black male flight attendant, who talks to her gently in Arabic. Her long headscarf is pure white.

The man beside me, named Bill Bryant, is from Oklahoma—an open-faced, cheerful oilman who has lived in Cairo for several years. I am immediately grateful for my time at the university in Norman. I know how to talk to this man; I am not put off, as I would once have been, by his easy self-assurance, his untroubled sense of belonging. We talk about Tulsa, Oklahoma City, the landscape near Lawton. I tell him how I grew to love his state. And he tells me of his love for Cairo and the Egyptians. "They have wonderful hearts," he says. "They may try to trick you, but they have wonderful hearts." He describes diving in the Red Sea, late-night outings into the desert to watch meteor showers, felucca rides on the Nile at sunset. Bill's Egypt is a vast playground, his life there one of unselfconscious enjoyment. Yet for all his casual aplomb, he has not lived only on the surface of things; his knowing respect for Egyptian people makes me trust and respect him. Before we disembark, we exchange telephone numbers; he tells me to call if I need anything.

◆

My heart beats wildly as I approach passport control. I've already walked a few hundred feet on Egyptian territory in the airport corridor, but this is, technically, the border. This is where I will be stopped, interrogated, locked away. On my U.S. passport it is plainly written, " Place of birth / *Lieu de naissance*: EGYPT." Won't they ask me what I'm doing here now? Won't they ask me why I left? Will they read my name and know that I am Jewish? Will they find me on a list of criminals? My parents left Egypt illegally just a year before the 1952 Revolution, having declared that they were taking a short vacation to Italy. When the official inspecting their bags found silver and jewelry among the tightly packed clothes, my father slipped him several one-pound notes. "Every time they found something, Felix gave them another pound," my mother has told me. Rugs, linens, photographs— for each item, a one-pound note. Swathed in layers of clothes and covered in jewelry, I was impervious to the details of this drama. But I imbibed its essence—my parents' paralyzing fear— magnifying it as I matured. At every border crossing to this day, I stiffen, cling to my passport, strive to make myself invisible.

And now I have come to the ultimate border, the original scene. Rigid with fear, I am certain no one will ever hear from me again. I don't know whether or not to make eye contact with the man behind the glass window. People in a long line shuffle along. The man takes each passport, scrutinizes it slowly, shows it to the man standing behind him. They confer in low tones, then nod, barely, as the first man hands the document back to the traveler. I await my turn in a tumult of anxiety. And then it happens.

I give the man my passport.

He peers at it blankly, then hands it back to me.

I am in.

That's all it takes. I give a man my passport, he looks at it, he gives it back.

I am stunned, breathless, thrilled. But there is no one with whom to share my joy, no one to hug or kiss, and so I do what everyone around me is doing: I walk onward toward the baggage claim area. Here, three Muslim men unroll a worn brown prayer rug beside the still-empty conveyor belt. They take off their shoes, step onto the rug, and begin a series of deep prostrations. I cannot tell whether they are performing one of the five daily prayers mandated by Islam or if this is a special prayer of homecoming, a formal expression of gratitude for safe landing. Whatever the nature of their rite, their actions mesmerize me, and I watch silently, envying their unselfconscious reverence. I want to make their gestures mine, to bend my knees and bow my head, to touch my forehead to this ground. Egypt. I have arrived in Egypt. Around me I hear voices. *"Ahlan wa sahlan!"* people are saying to their relatives and friends. "Welcome!" And in the distance I see the man from the Windsor Hotel, carrying a small sign with my name on it. Later, in the taxi, when I tell him that I am Jewish and that I was born here, he will smile broadly and touch my hand. "Welcome to your homeland," he will say in all sincerity in English. And then, exuberantly in Arabic, *"Ahlan wa sahlan!,"* here you are at home.

◆

"Don't sit in the front seat of taxis unless the driver is a woman," the *Lonely Planet* guide to Egypt warns solitary female travelers. So when the driver, who has introduced himself as Samir, invites me to sit beside him, I hesitate for a moment. "It's better this way," he says, opening the door, and I succumb. It would be rude to refuse. After all, I tell myself, Egyptians are known for their hospitality. The driver works for the hotel. I will be safe.

Samir steers me into the heart of the city. "In Cairo, we drive like fish," he says, bringing his fingers together and weaving his hand through the air the way a minnow might thread its way through a tangle of seaweed. There are no traffic lights that I can discern; I can see no logic to the swirl of these thousands of moving vehicles—cars, buses, bicycles, vans. Horns function as elbows do in a packed pedestrian crowd; cars spill into traffic circles like dried beans scattering from overturned canvas sacks. We pass Heliopolis, the elegant suburb where my parents once lived, now a crowded district of concrete high-rises; in the distance I see the ancient cemeteries known as Cities of the Dead. Samir points out the Khan al-Khalili, promising to bring me back the next day if I wish; after skirting the Mouski district, we come to Midan Ataba and Ezbekia Garden, not far from where the Royal Opera House once stood. Growing up, my mother had loved the old Opera House, which had been inaugurated with great pomp in 1871 for the opening of the Suez Canal. There she saw the Comédie-Française perform Molière; there she fell in love with *Madama Butterfly*. But that ornate edifice, a symbol of European dominance, burned to the ground in 1971; in 1988 it was replaced by a building in a modern Middle Eastern style, the new Cairo Opera House on the island of Gezira.

Just past Ezbekia, we turn into a small block-long street. I see a corner café, where old men share *sheesha* pipes at small outdoor tables; on the sidewalk, young boys behind a wooden crate offer low-cost shoe shines to passersby. Shoe shining is good business in Cairo, where street sweepers work long hours to keep the desert dust at bay. Samir leads me to the door of the Windsor; it opens into a tiny, busy lobby. I clamber over piles of luggage to the high desk in the rear. A large antique switchboard fills the wall beside it. They were expecting me, the clerk says; they are happy to see me. *Ahlan wa sahlan.* But I must wait. The manager will speak to me.

"Your room is not ready," the manager says apologetically when he arrives from his office on the second floor. "We are very sorry. We can give you a room in our sister hotel, but your room here is not ready right now."

I have been traveling for more than twenty-four hours, and I find it hard to grasp what I've just been told. My room is not ready? But I have a confirmed reservation. I had faxed the office again, just the day before.

"Of course," the manager assures me. "We have a room for you. But it is not ready yet. If you like, you can stay at the Pension Roma, just down the street."

But I was counting on the Windsor. All that research to pick just the right hotel!

"Can I wait?"

"Of course," the man assures me. "You can wait upstairs in the lounge. It will just be a little while."

I must be calm, I tell myself. It is no use to protest, and it will, after all, be good to sit. Leaving my bags behind the desk, I climb the worn marble staircase to the second floor.

In an instant, I know why my colleague recommended this place, why Samir called it, not the best bar in Cairo, but "the best bar in the world." The lounge is large, extending across the width of the building, with a golden wooden floor and numerous tall, recessed windows framed by faded muslin curtains. Low tables on worn Oriental rugs of various sizes serve as focal points for small groupings of caned armchairs and stiff-backed antique sofas; high above, ceiling fans slowly turn. To my surprise, the room has been decorated for Christmas—red and green tinsel streamers are draped from the ceiling, and a small artificial tree twinkles between two windows. The owners, I will later learn, are Copt, and Coptic Christmas is January 6, just a few days away. Behind the polished wooden bar, massive mirrors dimly reflect the late afternoon light. Groups of people are scattered throughout: a beautiful young woman tête-à-tête with an elderly Egyptian man; several Europeans huddled over maps; a solitary woman, reading. Good-looking young waiters in maroon vests and black bow ties stand beside the bar; among them is an older man in a red tarboosh and long white galabia, the traditional garment worn by Egyptian men.

I find a low chair and a small round table beside a window, sink down, order tea. It is delicious, black and strong, sweetened with a cube of sugar I dissolve by stirring with a tiny spoon that tinkles as it strikes the small white porcelain cup.

◆

Six hours later the manager comes to tell me that my room is ready. But I am by now unperturbed; the lounge of the Windsor Hotel has put me at ease. I have spent much of my time talking with a middle-aged Coptic journalist who offers to show me the city. He approached my table not long after I sat down, asking in English if he might speak with me. Later we were joined by a woman he knew, and we sat comfortably, like old friends, talking of the changes they had witnessed during their lives in Cairo.

Up two more flights of stairs and at the end of a long corridor, I find my room: high ceilinged, dark, and spare. A narrow bed, with a polished wooden headboard, flanks the far wall; to the right of the door, a small wooden desk; to the left, a sagging brown armchair; and in the corner, at an angle, a large wooden wardrobe. Dim pink and yellow flowers climb the papered walls; worn brown carpeting covers the floor. Behind a glass door on the right is a clean, white-tiled bathroom. Dropping my bags, I fall onto the bed. It is hard, resistant, with a scratchy wool blanket that smells like the ones I remember from childhood. Beside me, tall French windows open onto a narrow ledge guarded by a wooden rail—a mock balcony. Old wooden louvers cover the windows; over them hang heavy muslin curtains, thick with dust. Only a foreigner would want to open those windows. Outside, the air is filled with fumes and dust; inside, the room is cool and sweet, a dim sanctuary.

◆

In the morning, my friend Mervat meets me in the lounge. We had made these plans long in advance; for it is thanks largely to Mervat that I am here at all, that I have summoned the courage to make this long-contemplated return. A professor of political science at an American university, Mervat was born in Cairo—in a Muslim family—the same year as I; although she is now an American citizen, she returns each year to visit family and friends. When we met at a conference a few years ago and I told her that I was Egyptian, she called me "cousin"; when I confessed that I was also Jewish, she changed the appellation to "sister." I told her of my longing to visit Cairo and she promised to help. For each of us our friendship, and this journey, is an effort at reparation, an attempt to make amends for the historical forces that have separated and wounded each of our communities.

"You must learn to cross the street," Mervat tells me now, as we plunge into one of Cairo's main squares—not a square at all, but a swirling stream of traffic, a whirlpool, with a dozen tributaries hurtling in.

Halfway across I freeze. Horns blast on all sides.

"Walk," Mervat says firmly. "You must walk. Otherwise the drivers won't know what to do, and you will cause an accident. You must walk."

◆

It is Ramadan during my stay in Cairo and the city pulses with the rhythm of the holy fast. During the day, sixteen million people abstain from food or drink. By two or three each afternoon, the tension of their self-restraint is palpable; by four, the streets are filled with workers rushing to be home by sundown, when loudspeakers throughout the city announce the time for Iftar, the ceremonial meal to break the fast. On the streets, neighborhood restaurants offer free meals to the indigent, and, on busy downtown corners, groups spread rugs on the sidewalk, feasting on bread and *ful*. Later, far into the night, families stroll together through the city's streets, filling the cafés until just before dawn.

Because I will be spending so much time with Mervat— sharing Iftar with her family nearly every evening—I decide to keep the fast, albeit in my own way. Each morning, I take a small breakfast at the Windsor, and though I drink water freely throughout the day I do not eat any lunch or snacks. In this way I can approximate the experience of the other Egyptians I will be meeting, sharing in the great city's ebb and flow. In this way too, I imagine, I can expiate my parents' refusal to participate in the Muslim life that had surrounded them in Cairo, atone for their withdrawal from the culture within which they lived. "You mean you never ate in a Muslim's house?" I asked my mother again and again as a child. "No," she said, "we didn't know any Muslims."

◆

"How do you want me to introduce you?" Mervat asks me now, when we talk about the people I will be meeting—her sister and brother-in-law, her husband's family, friends she has known since childhood. She is concerned, not wanting my visit to be tainted by anti-Semitism or anti-Zionism. Some people, she admits, are still very hostile to Israel and to Jews.

"Tell them I am an American woman, Jewish, born in Egypt," I say. "Tell them I am an Egyptian Jew."

The first day, Mervat leads me to the Egyptian Museum and then to Coptic Cairo, the oldest part of the city, where she wants me to see the Ben Ezra Synagogue, dating from the ninth century, now lavishly restored in gold and lapis and coral. Nearby, I wander into a Coptic cemetery, where an old man shows me the tiny blue cross tattooed on his wrist. "*Wahid, wahid,*" he says when I manage to communicate that I am Jewish ("*Yahudia Masria,*" I have learned to say. "*Ana Yahudia Masria.*" "I am an Egyptian Jew"). The Copts and the Jews, he indicates, holding a finger of each hand side by side, are "*wahid, wahid,*"—one and one, together. His face beams as he calls me *habibti*—a word that takes me back to family gatherings in my parents' Brooklyn home. "*Habibti,*" my uncles used to call me. *Habibti*—sweetheart.

In the tiny Jewish library beside the synagogue, a young Muslim woman also welcomes me warmly. She cannot answer my questions about the current Jews of Egypt, nor even about the collection of antique Hebrew books it is her responsibility to guard, but she tells me I have arrived at a propitious moment. It is the annual festival of Abu Hassira, a Moroccan Jewish holy man buried in Egypt. Hundreds of Moroccan Jews from Israel are in Cairo this week to celebrate his *moulid*, his feast day. They will be gathering at Damanhour, a small village in the Delta, and they will also be visiting the Jewish sites in Cairo. Perhaps I can join them, she suggests. I have read about the Muslim custom of celebrating saint days with elaborate festivities; I did not know that Middle Eastern Jews venerated saints as well. *Wahid, wahid.*

◆

Before I left New Orleans, friends had shared with me whatever information they had about Cairo. One colleague gave me a photocopied page from a guide to Jewish travel in the Middle East. In the center of that sheet was a paragraph about the Jewish Community of Cairo, identifying its president as Carmen Weinstein and listing the phone number of the group. On my third day in the city, I decide to call.

"Who are you? Who gave you this number?" a rough voice asks when I introduce myself. "Why are you calling? Are you a journalist?"

Baffled, I try to explain: I am Jewish, born in Egypt. I have come back to explore the city of my origin, hoping to meet people who might remember my parents or tell me something about the life they might have lived there. I ask again if I might speak to Mrs. Weinstein.

"Are you sure you are not a journalist?" the voice challenges.

I admit that I am a writer, but that the object of my quest is entirely personal.

"Come to Weinstein's Stationery Store at 2:00 p.m. tomorrow," the voice commands. When I say I have no idea how to find the shop, I am told to go to the Adly Street Synagogue at 1:30, where, the voice promises, someone will meet me.

The Adly Street Synagogue, just around the corner from my hotel, is the large downtown synagogue my mother attended as a child, the place where she and my father were wed in 1945. Officially named Char Hashamayim, or "The Gates of Heaven," it has been familiarly known as the Temple Ismailia, after the neighborhood where it is located. A large, solidly built structure with marble columns, art deco lamps, and intricately wrought iron rails across the women's balcony, the Adly Street Synagogue is the only one of Cairo's remaining synagogues where services are still held—on the rare occasions when a minyan, the gathering of ten Jewish men necessary to hold public prayer, is assembled. I arrive at the appointed hour and am admitted by a uniformed guard; inside, I meet Mme Hazi, the elderly Yemenite Jew who serves as the synagogue's volunteer caretaker. I introduce myself in French, and we talk easily.

Soon it is time to lock up the synagogue for the afternoon, and the guard leads me to Weinstein's Stationery Store, just a few blocks away. There, I am directed to a chair—where I sit for more than an hour. The narrow shop is dark and cool. A long wooden counter lines one wall; opposite it, glassed-in shelves climb to the high pressed-tin ceiling. A middle-aged man and a young woman help customers, painstakingly writing out receipts by hand, in carbon-copy triplicate, and ringing up sales on an antique metal cash register. One well-dressed man spends thirty minutes selecting the paper for his business card; other people come in and quickly choose calendars, notebooks, pencils, pens. Standing in the back, Mme Weinstein—carefully dressed, well made up, strong featured—speaks on a black rotary phone.

At last, her business concluded, Mme Weinstein turns to me. "Who was your father?" she demands, and I recognize the voice that had questioned me the day before.

I tell her my father's name, but her face remains blank. I offer my mother's maiden name, Chalom; my father's mother's,

Beyda; my mother's mother's mother's, Sassoon. Still, Mme Weinstein is unmoved. I fear that she suspects me of being an impostor, a journalist planning to deceive her. What proof can I offer of the Egyptian Jewish origin I claim? Her doubt makes me wonder. What evidence *do* I have that I am who I say I am? Nothing more than my parents' fragmentary stories and still more fragmentary relics; nothing more than a few photographs, some jewelry, my great-grandmother's lace fan, to assure me of my birthplace; nothing but the shards of memory and loss.

But how, then, to account for this astonishing new sensation, the sensation I have had ever since stepping off the plane, that I am, for the first time in my conscious life, in a place I can unambiguously call home? Everywhere I look, dark eyes reflect mine; soft voices echo; gestures, accents, smiles all speak to me of a world I have always known, a landscape that has always been familiar. Even my skin seems to recognize and welcome the touch of the dry, light air. I switch from English to French as I struggle to explain myself to Mme Weinstein.

"Je suis venue içi," I tell her haltingly, "I have come here," *"pour me découvrir moi-même,"* "to discover myself." *"Je suis venue pour rencontrer des autres Juifs égyptiens; je veux connaître le pays de ma naissance."* "I have come in order to meet other Egyptian Jews; I want to know the country of my birth."

Mme Weinstein has seen others like me. She introduces me to her mother, Esther, who has just entered the shop. *"Ç'est la nostalgie,"* the older woman says dismissively. "It's nostalgia."

I protest that there is something more, but the Weinsteins remain impassive. They are among the handful of Jews who remained in Cairo through the revolution, through the years of anti-Zionism and anti-Semitism, through the 1967 war with Israel. What empathy can they have for those of us who chose to live in relative ease on the other side of the Atlantic, abandoning the country of their birth?

"But I was just a child," I say finally. "How can it be nostalgia if I have no memories? I am here to learn."

"If you want to meet the Jewish community here," Mme Weinstein finally relents, "come to the synagogue on Saturday morning. I will introduce you." And she makes another, more subtle offer, something I fear may be a test. "If you want to help us, come to the synagogue tomorrow at eleven."

Our interview over, she hands me a stack of photocopies, newsletters from the Jewish Community of Cairo. "You might want to read these," she says as she turns back to the business of her shop.

The next morning, just at eleven, I present myself to Mme Hazi at the synagogue. She is frantic, anticipating a busload of visitors from Israel—the Moroccan Jews here for the festival of Abu Hassira. "They are very difficult," she warns. When the bus arrives, dozens of men in dark coats and hats spill out, swarming through the synagogue, posing for photographs, demanding to see the Torahs Mme Hazi has locked away. "I do not have the key," she insists. The newsletters I read the night before have made it plain to me that these Torahs are the subject of much controversy and the cause of Mme Weinstein's caution with me and others. For in the past few years, Egyptian Jews from the United States and Israel have tried to remove these Torahs from Char Hashamayim, claiming them as their "patrimony." But Mme Weinstein has had the Torahs classified as Egyptian antiquities. They belong in Cairo, she insists, where they will one day become the focal point for a revitalized Jewish community. As she said in a recent interview, "Our community is indeed shrinking—but dying? I don't believe it will ever die." With Mme Hazi, I try to keep the men away from the treasures of Char Hashamayim. At one point, they accuse me of desecrating the sanctuary: I am a woman in a space reserved for men. Surely they are the ones violating the sanctity of the synagogue, I try to tell them.

Later that afternoon, I join Mervat. Our plan is to do some shopping in the Khan al-Khalili and then go on to the adjacent Mouski neighborhood, where I hope to find yet another synagogue, the Rambam, the "illustrious" synagogue of Moses Maimonides, familiarly known as Rav Moshe. The Rambam is "not on any tourist itinerary," I have learned from my photocopied guide to Jewish travel—and, apparently, not on any map either. Yet I feel compelled to find it. I know something of Maimonides' renown, something of his life in Egypt, where he served as physician to Salah al-Din and was venerated as a sage. But how to locate the synagogue he had established, the yeshiva where he had taught? No one can offer any precise information. "It's on the Darb Mahmoud," a young American student working with Mme Weinstein tells me, "an alley in the Mouski." But where exactly is the Darb Mahmoud? He can't say. "Just go to the Mouski and ask."

Now, Mervat and I, laden with cumbersome bags—we have henna and cumin and dried figs, an embroidered galabia and a tooled-leather pouf—venture into the Mouski, an ancient market area where sheep and chickens wander between motorbikes and small trucks, where crumbling buildings seem ready to fall in upon narrow, broken streets.

Mervat speaks for me, asking one male shopkeeper after another if he can direct us to the Darb Mahmoud. The answer—"Go down that way, turn left, then ask again"—is invariable. Each shopkeeper ponders Mervat's question, points, then turns away. There are customers to serve, neighbors with whom to chat. At each stopping point, Mervat asks again, selecting someone in a doorway or beside a sack of spices, someone who seems not too disconcerted by our obviously Western clothes and uncovered, cropped hair. For here in the Mouski, people are all in traditional garb. Men wear galabias and the women's hair is covered; we cannot hide the fact that we are strangers, intruders in this ancient district. What are we doing looking for an old synagogue on this hot Ramadan afternoon? As we continue to walk, apparently in circles, we begin to worry. At one bewildering junction, Mervat asks a man, "Left? Are you sure? Couldn't it be right?" He looks at her with a weary smile. "Left, right, what's the difference?, " he shrugs. "Suit yourself."

"I don't think anyone knows where it is," Mervat confesses to me then. "They're just saying something to placate us. It's an Egyptian custom."

"OK," I say. "Let's turn back. It's not that important anyway. Let's go back to the Khan al-Khalili."

"No," Mervat says stubbornly, "we're not going back. We've come this far, and we're going to find it."

Sweating in the heat, exhausted from her fast, Mervat refuses to abandon the quest. She is more committed than I am, determined to lead me to this abandoned old synagogue. It has become for her a matter of pride, a test of Egyptian hospitality. For she too, like me, is engaged in an effort of expiation.

And so we continue, walking fifty feet, stopping, asking, walking fifty feet again. By now I have completely lost whatever geographic orientation I might once have had. I cannot say where north, south, east, or west is: The sun is not visible in the hazy sky, and the district's ancient buildings and labyrinthine streets have become my entire world, crowding out all perception of the twentieth century. Even the sounds have changed: the heavy roar of traffic quelled, the din of modernity stilled. We are in the district that was once called *harat al-yahud*, the medieval Jewish quarter, and here and there I glimpse a familiar name— Cohen or Levy or Setton—faded yet still evident above a shop where multicolored bolts of fabrics tower above wooden tables. All around me, amid the busy merchants and shoppers, I see beggars dragging themselves on blackened limbs, barefoot children playing beside piles of dung, ragged animals roaming hungrily. I want to flee, yet at the same time I am enthralled. Looking into the eyes of beggars and children and shoppers and shopkeepers, I sense that I have somehow reached a place where all difference is reconciled, where privation coexists with prosperity, where youth and age, male and female, animal and human, all share a common life—transient, eternal. Time seems to stop here in this place where I cannot separate myself from all that I see—the old man and the young woman; the buyer and the seller; the dying, the just being born.

And then, as if within a dream, I glimpse a bare white dome, arcing above a yellow wall.

"There," I whisper to Mervat, touching her shoulder and turning her so that she might see. "There."

"Where?" she asks, and I know she does not share my vision. We move to a small step in front of a shop, and I direct her gaze.

"There." I point again.

The building is small, with padlocked wooden doors and faded walls. Now Mervat can see the dome, but she is unconvinced. "There's no sign," she says, "no mark on the building, nothing to show it was a synagogue."

Still, I am certain. This was a place of Jewish worship. Are we in the Darb Mahmoud, then? Have we found the Rambam? As I wonder, a well-dressed man in Western clothes suddenly appears. Are we lost, he asks in Arabic? Mervat explains our quest, and I watch as the man's face opens. "Yes," he tells her, this building *was* an old synagogue, but not the Rambam. The Rambam is just around the corner, beside the old Coptic church, whose spire is visible behind us. Barely pausing to thank him, we hurry around the next turn.

◆

The plain, low building extends along a vacant, garbage-strewn alley, the Darb Mahmoud. At the head of the alley, two young Egyptian soldiers, holding rifles across their chests, eye us suspiciously. Mervat asks if we might enter the street, and reluctantly, they let us through. Mervat stays beside them, while I walk toward the synagogue. A tablet with the ten commandments is carved above the main entrance; beside it, I see the name of Moses ibn Maimoun engraved in Hebrew and Arabic. The door is locked, the roof fallen in, the walls decayed. On tiptoe, I peer through iron grates into the sanctuary, see broken steps and crumbling walls, a worn bimah where the Sefer Torah once rested.

The Rambam is a ruin, locked against human entrance yet open to wind and rain. For a moment, the desolation of this place assails me, and in a sudden spasm, I begin to cry. Watching me suspiciously, the soldiers grow alarmed. They have been told to wait for the Abu Hassira pilgrims, and they are unsettled by our presence. "Why is she crying?" one of them asks Mervat. She explains that I am an Egyptian Jew, born in Cairo, returning after fifty years.

"We must do what is right by her," he says, shaking his head. "Let her cry."

And so I cry, hot steady tears rising from within, as if I have stumbled upon an ancient spring that flows upward from the stones, through my body, and back onto the stones again. Mervat and the soldiers discreetly turn away, respecting what they imagine to be my suffering. But these are not exactly tears of pain. Mervat's answer to the soldier is good as far as it goes, but it does not go far enough. I am crying, no doubt, for the history of the Jews in modern Egypt, for our community's dislocation, for my family's losses, and for my own. I am crying for the Rambam, for the sadness inherent in the abandonment and decay of this once vital center of worship. But my tears have their source elsewhere, in a place I cannot name or understand. I sense that they embody gain as well as loss. For, once again, I have the sensation of homecoming: here, in this garbage-strewn alley, beside the broken windows and graffiti-covered walls, everything seems finally to cohere. I want to sink onto the stones, to rest, at peace. But the Abu Hassira pilgrims are on their way, and Mervat and I are expected for dinner downtown.

Much later that night, alone in my room at the Windsor, I dream of Jewish stars, thousands of Jewish stars gleaming above me on an inlaid dome, mother-of-pearl and ebony and gold; at its center, I see a face, an ancient Jewish man's face, gazing calmly down. When I awake, startled, long before dawn, I rummage through my papers to see if I can learn anything more about the Rambam. What *is* this place I have found? In one of Mme Weinstein's newsletters, I read her mother's words. Calling herself an "adept of *Rav Moshe*," Esther writes that Maimonides' "warm presence" is always palpable to her on Darb Mahmoud. "Some of you will understand what I mean," she continues, "for like myself and several others who suffered from various illnesses, we dreamed of Ben Maimon who advised us silently of the cure we should follow."

So, I conclude, the Rambam was a place of healing as well as a place of worship. Maimonides was, after all, both a noted doctor and a gifted scholar, serving as the personal physician of the twelfth-century sultan Salah al-Din. His healing powers must have been localized in his synagogue after his death. His spirit, hovering over the Rambam, answers the prayers of the devout. *That* must have been why I cried, I tell myself: I must have sensed Maimonides' energy. Satisfied, I slip into sleep, still covered by a dome of stars.

At Char Hashamayim the next morning, a service is in progress. The synagogue is filled with the Abu Hassira pilgrims—men on the ground floor, women in the balcony. When an ancient Torah is removed from the ark, there is jubilation, the women ululating, throwing tiny wrapped candies onto the bimah.

"I don't know if it's ever been this full since the forties," Mme Weinstein tells me.

After the service, I sit with a small group of women in the synagogue's courtyard.

"We're glad you have come," several women say to me. *"Ahlan wa sahlan."*

◆

Back in the States, I enthusiastically recount my trip to my parents.

"Do you know the Rambam Synagogue—the one in the Mouski section?" I ask, certain that the answer will be no. The Mouski had been a lower-class Jewish neighborhood, and I imagined that my middle-class parents, living in Ismailia or Heliopolis, would not have gone there.

"Of course we knew it," my father answers, annoyed. Despite the haze caused by his Parkinson's, he recognizes my arrogance. "Everybody knew it."

"People went there to get healed," my father's cousin Sheila, visiting Florida for the winter, says. "It was very famous, very popular. You would sleep in a little room, and hope for a dream that would answer your prayer. Maimonides would come to you in a dream. Everybody went—Jews, Arabs, Christians."

My mother recalls an incident: "*Tante* Suze spent a night there when she was a girl. She was very sick, and nothing could make her better, so her family took her there."

"Was she healed?" I ask.

"Yes," my mother admits, "she got better."

Suddenly my father is looking keenly across the table at my mother. The sparkle in his eye has returned; he is clear, focused, bright.

"You slept there too," he says. "You slept there. You spent the night there, when you were hoping to have a baby. You went with your mother."

"I don't remember," my mother says defensively. "I don't remember going there."

"I remember it vividly," my father says again. "You spent the night there when you were waiting to get pregnant."

My mother says she doesn't remember, but my father is certain. It was after her miscarriages, the year before I was born. She had gone to the Rambam with her mother, spent the night, prayed for a successful pregnancy. It was late in 1948, the year the state of Israel was established. She would have walked through the Mouski with her mother, my *Nonna*, threaded her way through its labyrinthine streets, entered a small room beside the main sanctuary, settled onto a straw pallet, lain there through the night, waiting, praying, seeking an answering dream.

"When storms and tempests threatened us," Maimonides wrote in 1167, "we used to wander from place to place." And, he concluded, "We have now been enabled to find here a resting place." He was writing about the Jewish community's discovery of a safe haven in medieval Cairo. Citing a verse from Micah, he continued, "I will seek the lost one, and that which has been cast out I will bring back, and the broken one I will cure."

I never located, on my first trip back to Cairo, my mother's apartment on rue Suleiman Pasha or the Heliopolis neighborhood where I spent my first days. What I found, instead, was the ancient home of dreams—a resting place, a cure.

Ten: And Then　　　◆　◆　◆

We shall not cease from exploration
And the end of all our exploring
Will be to arrive where we started
And know the place for the first time.
—T. S. Eliot, "Little Gidding"

The summer before the storm, I traveled again to Cairo, accompanied this time by a law professor who lived in New York and ran a summer program in Egypt. We had met three

Joyce Zonana on Venus Street, New Orleans, 2003.

years earlier on a train, and I had been drawn to him by his voice, his words in Arabic, his familiarity with and love for the ancient streets. A tempest in my life followed. When I was most uncertain about the outcome—where I would live and how or with whom, I bought a small piece of land on the north shore of Lake Pontchartrain—three acres in the woods near Folsom, across the road from the Little Tchefuncte River and adjacent to the property of Medicine Hawk and Mary Ann, the friends who had introduced me to Native American ceremony. If I had nothing else, I reasoned, I would have this small piece of earth, a place I could call home.

After a year of struggle, Kay and I parted in sorrow. We sold the house on Bayou St. John we had shared for five years, and I found another one, a three-bedroom craftsman's cottage on a quiet street in Gentilly Terrace, the first twentieth-century neighborhood in the United States to become a National Register Historic District. From my earliest days in New Orleans, I had been drawn to this small area of California-style bungalows built between 1910 and 1940 on some of the highest ground in the city. The meticulously restored house I chose seemed ideal, with its golden oak floors, arched doorways, and cove ceilings. For the first time in my adult life, I had a formal dining room and a screened porch, like the one I remembered at Mrs. Rosenblum's house in Brooklyn; in the kitchen, built-in wood-and-glass cabinets complemented an antique Chambers stove. My friend and colleague Lynn lived on the next block, and Sarah, a retired professor of art history who was transforming her front lawn into a captivating tangle of flowers and fruit, dwelt across the way. The neighbors, many of whom had lived on the street since childhood, smiled and stopped to talk each morning; the trees—a Southern magnolia, two figs, a holly, an oak, a chinaberry, and an elder—shaded my dreams.

With my share of the profit from selling the last house, I was able to buy, not only this new home, but also the solid furniture I had begun to long for: a large round dining table with inlaid mahogany veneer, a plush maroon velvet sofa, a heavy wooden bed. I had wood-frame screens constructed for all the windows and ceramic tiles laid in the kitchen and on the porch. On the walls I hung my treasures: an antique lace fan that had belonged to my great-grandmother, a tiny needlepoint image of feluccas on the Nile stitched by my maternal *Tante* Diane. Wool rugs I had purchased on a trip to Turkey, handmade lace tablecloths from Greece, the beautiful silver trays my mother had received at her wedding—all contributed to my sense of being fully at home, *chez moi*. A year after I moved in, I adopted two orange tabby kittens, littermates who became my new companions.

Psychologists say that the places we gravitate toward in adulthood mirror those we knew in childhood, and it may be that what drew me to 4617 Venus Street was its similarity to the Heliopolis apartment where I spent my earliest days. Recently, my mother spoke of that apartment: its long corridor and large rooms, its sense of air and space—the very things I had on Venus Street. She too loved my Gentilly cottage, calling it a "real home." The formal dining room made us both especially happy, recalling as it did the generous space my maternal grandmother had maintained for so many years on the rue Suleiman Pasha in Cairo. Like her, I invited people often, hosting small dinner parties, large gatherings, and celebrations for all the holidays, Jewish and otherwise.

One gentle spring afternoon, coming back to the house after celebrating Mother's Day—we had drunk mimosas and danced to a traditional jazz band at one of the city's grand old downtown hotels—my mother and I made stuffed grape leaves together. I had invited the students in my Victorian literature seminar to a small end-of-semester party; I had promised to make them this delicacy. So, with unaccustomed ease, for the first time in my life, it seemed, I cooked alongside my mother. With the windows open and the sweet air wafting in, we chopped and mixed and rolled and simmered. We talked and laughed and reminisced. On the way back to my house after brunch, we had stopped at one of the plant nurseries in the city, searching for the night-blooming jasmine she remembered from Cairo. Although we hadn't found it, our walk among the brightly colored flowers brought us both to quiet reverie. The hours in my kitchen passed quickly as we worked together.

I saw Bernard—the man I had met on the train—fitfully, managing occasional trysts in New York, New Orleans, Cairo, Vermont. But I remained deeply conflicted about separating from Kay, missing her terribly, and ashamed of my violation of her trust and of the very public breakup of our very public relationship. We *had* been fighting bitterly for many months before I met Bernard, and I *had* been unhappy for several years before then, but my betrayal of her could not be construed as anything other than a betrayal. I imagined students—especially the young lesbians who had looked up to us—turning against me; and I was sure that many of our gay colleagues and friends regarded me with disdain. Sleeping with a man after more than twenty years with women was harder to come to terms with than coming out as a lesbian had been. Not only was I stepping outside the norms of a community, this time it was a community I had chosen and publicly embraced, a marginalized community that demanded and deserved my ongoing solidarity. To make things worse, I was leaving a woman I still loved. I could not make a clean break. Not unsurprisingly, Bernard found it difficult to sustain his end of our arrangement. But in the summer of 2005 he invited me to join him for a cruise up the Nile, and I agreed to go. Luxor, the Valley of the Kings, the Temple of Isis—I clambered around the ancient sites, trying to find my heart.

When I returned in early August, I busied myself preparing for the new semester. I would be teaching ancient Greek literature and philosophy as always, along with a creative-writing workshop for the first time. I had also decided to put myself up for promotion to full professor. To that end, I assembled files and wrote a career narrative, documenting my accomplishments and arguing that I had internally arrived at the status for which I now sought external affirmation. It had taken me twenty years of full-time teaching to reach that point—longer than for most, perhaps, yet right for me. Odysseus's journey, I told myself, the twenty years of battle and self-mastery. Feeling especially comfortable about my work, I rearranged my study and settled into two writing projects: an essay on Betty Smith's *A Tree Grows in Brooklyn*, and an article about four contemporary Egyptian Jewish narratives of exile and homecoming. The storm, arising suddenly in the Gulf, was an annoying interruption, something I was sure I had no time for.

It wasn't as if I hadn't evacuated for hurricanes before. For Andrew in 1992, for Georges in 1998, and for Ivan in 2004, I had packed the car and driven frantically into the night—to Mississippi, to Alabama, to Arkansas, to wherever I could find a motel with room for me, the cats, and my traveling companion of the moment (my partner Ruth in 1992, Kay in 1998, my mother in 2004). During my first year in New Orleans, a colleague, an environmental sociologist whose specialty was disaster planning, had persuaded me that the "disaster scenario"—Lake Pontchartrain overtopping the levees; the city inundated with ten feet of water for weeks; hundreds, perhaps thousands, of people dead—was a very real possibility. Because of the paucity of evacuation routes, Shirley insisted that one had to leave seventy-two hours before a major storm, and I believed her. Many years earlier, while still on the East Coast, I had read Zora Neale Hurston's *Their Eyes Were Watching God*, a novel that evokes, in terrifying detail, the 1928 hurricane that devastated central Florida. Hurston's portrayal of humans and animals struggling to escape the rapidly rising water never left me; whenever a storm threatened Louisiana I thought of the Native Americans in Florida who, well before the 1928 storm, followed the birds away from the low-lying lands around Lake Okeechobee. Like them, I didn't want to be caught unawares.

But when news of Katrina filtered into my consciousness that last weekend of August 2005, I was less than eager to take off. Late Friday night, after sharing a long, relaxed dinner with

Lynn—I had made lentil soup and salad, and we had lingered over coffee and fruit—I checked my e-mail before going to bed. I found a note from a friend in New Hampshire, a former New Orleanian.

"What are you planning to do about Katrina?" she asked.

"Nothing," I typed quickly in reply. The name of the storm— threatening Florida, the last I heard—had not even registered before that moment. "Do I need to do anything?"

Still, I visited the National Weather Service website before turning in, noting the unusually high probability (17 percent) assigned to the storm's making landfall within seventy-five miles of New Orleans. But probabilities were not actualities. I told myself that things would change. Medicine Hawk and Mary Ann and I were intending to build and dedicate a small sweat lodge on my Folsom land on Saturday. We had been preparing for months: Hawk had cleared the space and, with Mary Ann's great-grandson Dylan, had gathered the willows; I had assembled a pile of old blankets to use as a covering; Mary Ann had been saying prayers at the site for several days. We were going to gather early on Saturday and spend the whole day together. Afterward, on Sunday, I would write a new lecture on Books 9–12 of the *Odyssey*; although I taught the poem every year and had a standard lecture prepared, I wanted to reread the section carefully and come up with something new. Evacuation was not part of my weekend plans.

At 9:30 a.m. on Saturday, just as I was slicing the fresh honeydew melon for the fruit salad I was preparing to bring across the lake, Mary Ann called.

"Have you turned on the TV this morning?" she asked.

"No, should I?"

"I think so," she said. "They say there's a very big storm in the Gulf, and Hawk thinks we need to prepare the house. We'll have to build the lodge another time."

I was disappointed, but still not alarmed. Mary Ann's news helped me to understand why my next-door neighbors had been loading the car so early in the morning, driving off before 9:00 a.m. They had small children and had a house to go to in Mississippi. They always left at the first hint of danger. That didn't mean I needed to. But, after speaking with Mary Ann, I walked across the street to consult Sarah.

"I'm staying," she said, before I could even ask. "I don't want to spend hours on the road for no reason." Last year, evacuating for Ivan, it had taken her twenty-one hours to get to Houston.

I returned to my house and turned on the TV. Images of the already enormous storm loomed—photos and graphics, projected paths. The newscasters had begun their frantic commentary, and traffic was already backed up as thousands of people lined up to leave. The governor had declared a state of emergency, and FEMA director Michael Brown was urging New Orleans residents to evacuate in anticipation of what he called "a very significant event." Yet somehow, things did not seem as bad to me as they had before Georges, when the Category 4 hurricane threatened to come directly up the Mississippi River—the true disaster scenario. Katrina was still only a Category 3.

I called Kay. She remained my closest friend in the city. "You need to leave," she said firmly. "This is the big one. You need to leave."

I was shocked by her certainty.

Seven years earlier we had fought bitterly in the hours before Georges. I had wanted to go. She had wanted to stay. In the end she had acceded to me, sitting sullenly for eight hours as I drove in terror toward Tallahassee. It turned out to be a false alarm.

"Are *you* leaving?" I asked.

"Yes," she said, "absolutely. You know I don't like to go, but I have a bad feeling about this one. I think this is the big one."

The big one. For years all of us in the city had talked about it, worried, made our plans. Could this be it? I didn't want to think so. I told Kay I would consider what she had said, and I picked up my Homer, turning to Book 9, the beginning of Odysseus's adventures:

Now Zeus who masses the stormclouds hit the fleet
with the North Wind—
        a howling, demonic gale, shrouding over
in thunderheads the earth and sea at once—
           and night swept down
from the sky and the ships went plunging headlong on,
our sails slashed to rags. . . .

The phone rang. It was my friend Deedy in Lafayette.

"Bill and I want you to come and stay with us," she said. "Bill's mother has a small house in the back with plenty of room for you and the cats."

For a moment I didn't know what she was talking about.

"But I'm not planning to go anywhere," I said.

"Well, the house is here," Deedy said. The year before, she had berated herself for not having thought to offer it to me during Ivan, when I had evacuated at the last minute with my mother. Unable to find a motel room any closer, we had driven more than five hundred miles to a small town in Arkansas, just across the river from Memphis, Tennessee. Two days later we had returned, exhausted. Not long after, my mother was hospitalized with a severe bronchial infection. "We'd love to have you, your mother, your cats," Deedy was now telling me.

"I'll call you if I decide to evacuate," I said.

I turned on the TV again, went to the weather service website, made some more phone calls.

Mary Lou next door was staying. "This house has been through Betsy and Camille," she told me. "If it's my time to die, I'll die. But I'll die here. I'm not going anywhere."

Down the street, Lynn was staying. The chair of my department, Peter, who lived a few blocks away and with whom just a few weeks earlier I had discussed the "disaster scenario" over wine and cheese, was staying. Charlotte, a former student and native New Orleanian who also lived in the neighborhood, was not budging. "Don't be silly," she said. "I never leave."

But as the morning passed, the storm kept getting bigger and the probabilities for a direct hit kept getting higher. Around noon, I went out to fill my car's gastank and to buy gallon bottles of water, still not sure what I would do, but wanting to have options. Long lines at the gas station and empty shelves at the grocery store helped convince me that other people in the neighborhood were concerned as well. They were taking the storm seriously, but most were planning to stay: They were simply stocking up, preparing to spend a few days without power in their homes. I began to bring things in from the yard and to clear the front porch. I got out the ax I had bought before Georges, to break through the roof, just in case. The air was heavy and still, the streets silent and tense. I remembered my policy, formulated earlier in the summer in an effort to avoid the agonizing that had paralyzed me in the past: Be safe, not sorry. Was this the time to apply it? At one thirty, Mayor Nagin appeared on TV. "This is not a test," he said. "This is the real deal." He had used similar words last year before Ivan. But he seemed grimmer this time. "Things could change, but as of right now, New Orleans is definitely the target for this hurricane," he said.

I made my decision. I called my mother. "We need to go," I said.

"I'm not going anywhere," she replied. "They're going to take care of us here." The management of her retirement community, Woldenberg Village, had assured the residents that they would be safe on the second floor of their sturdy, newly built, brick assisted-living facility. There were generators, bottles of water, plenty of food. "We'll be fine," my mother said.

I tried to persuade her to join me, but she was adamant. She had had enough last year. And she really didn't believe in the disaster scenario I kept telling her about. "The snakes and the dead bodies," I reminded her. "Do you really want to be here with the snakes and the dead bodies?"

She laughed. "Don't be foolish, Joyce. I'm staying."

Reluctantly, I allowed her to have her way, though I insisted that she refill her prescriptions that afternoon.

"I'll get them at Wal-Mart on Monday," she told me.

"There won't be a Wal-Mart on Monday," I said, and she laughed again.

Still, although I wasn't entirely persuaded that this was "the big one," I knew I didn't want to be alone in my house discovering that it was. I called my friend Christine. She also lived by herself, and had wanted to leave, but was reluctant to travel alone. I suggested we go together, and she agreed. I called other single women I knew and encouraged them to join us. But they were all planning to stay. I gathered up my laptop, hard copies of my writing projects, my jewelry, my insurance papers, and my passport. I put the cats in their carrier and called Deedy, telling her to expect us around midnight.

◆

Two days later I sat on Deedy's sofa, sobbing. The water in the city was rising and I couldn't reach my mother. Communication with Woldenberg Village was impossible. I tried calling the Red Cross, the police, the state troopers; there was either no answer or no information. On television we saw looting, fires, desperate people on rooftops and in the streets. How could I have left my mother behind to endure all this? What had become of her? I thought about driving back to the city to find her—but the roads were already blocked by the National Guard, and how would I manage to make my way if I *did* get through? I called *Tante* Suze in Florida and wept. Suze assured me I had done the right thing. But I refused to believe her. I should have made my mother come with me, or I should have stayed at her side. What kind of a daughter was I? My mother had Alzheimer's. Shouldn't I have been the one to make the decision and enforce it? My brother in New York and I frantically texted each other—although my cell phone didn't work for calls, I could send and receive text messages—but there was little we could do. Another long day and a half passed.

It wasn't just the unknown fate of my mother that had me in its grip. It was the fate of an entire community. Both Christine and I worried about the friends we had left behind, the people who had insisted on staying. The TV offered horrifying images of suffering—the Superdome, the Convention Center, the streets of the Ninth Ward and Lakeview. Although it was rarely mentioned by the newscasters, it was clear to us that the London Avenue Canal, in the center of my Gentilly neighborhood, had also been breached. Where were my friends Audrey and Charlotte, my neighbor Mary Lou? What about the family across the street who had been boarding up their windows when I left, determined to stay? What about Peter? Lynn, I knew, had left on Sunday morning after I called and insisted she go immediately. Sarah had left the night before. But the others?

Like the Greek warriors dispersed by wind and wave after the Trojan War, Christine and I sought news of our friends and neighbors. The returning Greeks had relied on tales told by other travelers, people who might have briefly glimpsed—or heard stories about—their companions. We turned to electronic sources—cell phones and the Internet—to gather news. For the most part it was hearsay, tales told and retold. Late in the week I learned from a website that Audrey had been "last seen at the New Orleans airport"; Charlotte, I discovered from a message board much later, had made her way to her daughter in Atlanta. Mary Ann called me from a motel in Arkansas; she had obtained my number from a mutual friend in Houston. Medicine Hawk had stayed behind in Folsom to take care of the house. Mary Ann was frantic for news of him, but of course there was none.

On Wednesday night, nearly three full days after the storm had made landfall, I stumbled on a clue about my mother. Someone, somewhere, had created an online discussion group for "friends and family of Woldenberg Village"; my brother had found it while searching the web and we had each signed on.

Using Deedy's computer, I obsessively checked my e-mail every hour. There was a rumor that the Woldenberg Village residents were being evacuated to Texas. No one knew for sure. But around 11:00 p.m., someone wrote with certainty: They were going to Methodist Hospital in Houston. He included a phone number. I called immediately. The calm, sweet-voiced woman on the other end could offer no information, but she patiently took all my numbers—my (nonworking at the moment) cell phone's, Deedy's, Christine's. A few moments later I called again, having realized I should also give her Deedy's land line.

"What is your mother's name?" she asked.

"Nelly Zonana."

"We just checked her in," she said. "She's here."

I had no idea of my mother's condition, no idea how she had withstood the days of deprivation and fear, the difficulties of the drive. But at least I knew where she was, and that she was alive—for now.

I texted my brother and told him to meet me in Houston.

The next morning we found her, shaken but cheerful, settled with several of her Woldenberg Village neighbors in a retirement community on the northwest side of Houston, concerned that she had lost her small suitcase, that the only thing she had to wear was the long flowered housedress she had on, that she had misplaced her medication. The day after we found one another, my mother flew back to New York with my brother; I returned to Lafayette, where I would spend another night before heading North.

Later my mother would confess that the windows in the purportedly safe building in which they had been sheltering had shattered; that she had watched a neighboring apartment complex crumple; that she heard gunshots from the street where the Wal-Mart was; that the supposedly abundant water and food supplies had quickly been exhausted. Three people died on the bus trip to Houston, and several were now critically ill. But she was fine, my mother kept saying when we were reunited.

There had been nothing for us to worry about. She was fine. And indeed, her experience and mine of Katrina were far less devastating than those of so many other people in the city. We were among the lucky ones, insulated from the worst of the suffering by our economic and racial privilege.

◆

The last class I had taught at the University of New Orleans, on the Friday before the storm, was a small discussion section with the students in the Greek literature course. Our subject was Books 5 through 8 of the *Odyssey*, and I had just introduced the concept of guest-friendship, *xenia*. "This was how a civil society was maintained," I explained. "Even if you didn't know who a traveler was, you welcomed him or her—offering a bath, fresh clothing, and food, even before asking his or her name; that person, in turn, would welcome other strangers."

"No way!" my students protested. "No one would do that these days!"

"They only did it because they thought strangers might be gods in disguise," several of them scoffed. "They only did it because they were afraid of punishment."

"Not exactly," I said. "They did it because it made sense."

I tried to persuade them that reciprocal hospitality might be motivated by something other than fear, that in an age without credit cards or hotels, it was a sensible way of holding together a far-flung island society—that it was indeed, as the Greeks believed, a mark of civilization. One of the names for Zeus, Xenios, identified him as the god of hosts and guests. For the Greeks, hospitality was an aspect of divinity, not so much a custom rooted in human fear of the gods as one that revealed the godliness of humans. My students' cynicism troubled me, and I resolved to work over the weekend to find a way to help them with this important concept. How could I have known that in a few days we would all be learning firsthand about the blessings of guest-friendship?

Christine and I had been welcomed warmly by Deedy's in-laws, the Hayses, late on Saturday night. "Here's the shower," they said. "Here's the kitchen, and some food you might want. Here are beds." The next morning, we left the cottage to make room for two families Mrs. Hayes knew from her church; we moved into Deedy's crowded house. I took an air mattress on the floor of the small study and Christine took the couch. We kept the cats locked in the study, away from Deedy and Bill's numerous dogs and cats. Five days later we were in Alabama staying with another family; next, we spent a night with friends of mine in Greensboro; finally, after two tense weeks on the road, I dropped Christine off in Virginia and went on to Brooklyn—where the daughter of a friend greeted me with fresh clothes, dinner, another comfortable bed, and a space for my wonderfully adaptable, patient cats. Along the way, in Alabama, we had come to a highway rest stop where the local community had organized a welcome center, offering food, clothes, toiletries.

Xenia, I kept thinking, *xenia*. What would we have done without it? And where were my skeptical students now? Were they and their families safe? Had any of them succumbed to the storm? I worried for them; I dreamed of them. Would I ever see them again? The class had gotten off to such a good start, with strong and vigorous discussion. Many of the students were from poor New Orleans families, families that would have been unable to leave, or would have resisted fleeing the storm. Had they stayed? Or were they scattered throughout the South, sleeping in strange beds? Were they, like me, thinking obsessively about Odysseus?

For in those tumultuous days following the storm, when I wasn't watching TV in horror or driving in panic, I was, in fact, thinking about the *Odyssey*, thinking that now I understood, now I knew what it was to lose your companions, what it was to be at the mercy of Poseidon and Zeus, gods of sea and storm; now I knew what it was to need to tell my story, to listen to those of others; now I understood why Odysseus sat on the shoreline "wrenching his heart with sobs and groans and anguish, / gazing out over the barren sea through blinding tears."

◆

The storm impelled me forward—or was it back?—to New York. As one friend put it while I debated which way to go, "It's hard to know whether going forward is going back or if going back is going forward." Should I return to New Orleans? Or should I "return" to New York? Which way would bring fulfillment? There seemed no easy answer, no clear path. Lafayette—a city I had never cared for—seemed suddenly appealing, too; for a few days I thought I might look for an apartment, join Deedy's gym, and work as a teacher of children from New Orleans. But I found myself driving toward New York, knowing that with each mile I traveled, I was moving psychically as well as physically away from my newly grown southern roots.

David Schoen, a Jungian analyst practicing on the north shore of Lake Pontchartrain, argues in the *Divine Tempest: The Hurricane as a Psychic Phenomenon*, that the hurricane—as a psychic symbol and real-world event—connects us with what Jungians call the "Self." It is a force that "humbles the human ego and highlights our ultimate dependence upon the divine"; like the mandala, the hurricane symbol arises "at a time in the individuation process where one is confronted with conscious decisions that will chart the fundamental course of life for good or bad." I had read Schoen's book before Katrina, and I thought of it often as I fled. Driving east on I-20, and then north on 95, was I charting the fundamental course of my life? Was it for good or ill? How would I know? "'Way leads on to way,'" Kay reminded me a few months later, when I called her for advice. "Robert Frost tells us his choice makes 'all the difference,' but he doesn't tell us what that difference is. He doesn't tell us if it was the right choice."

I drove to New York because that's where my mother and my brother and my goddaughter, Kiki, the daughter of *Tante* Suze's daughter, Colette, were. I knew that Gentilly Terrace was under six feet of water—the levee break in the London Avenue Canal having inundated the area—and that it would be several weeks before I could return, and to what? It was impossible to know. Did I have a job? Did I have a house? What about all the friends I still hadn't heard from? What would become of the city? I had always known that New Orleans was unstable, and, perversely, I had reveled in that instability. "When you live here," I exultingly told my East Coast friends, "you are forced to be aware of the transience of human civilization." The termites might consume your home; the floodwaters might fill the streets. Nature would triumph. Once, I walked along Lake Pontchartrain after a torrential rain. The lakefront roadway was closed; flocks of waterbirds waded through newly formed ponds beside the levee. "This is what the city will look like one day," I thought. "The swamp will return."

Yet when the moment arrived, I was as little prepared as anyone else, my bravura drowned with the city itself. Like so many others of us who had made it our home, I was grief-stricken, as well as angry, frightened, shocked. But because I had never fully *believed* in the city, I was willing, perhaps too willing, to let it go. I had always told myself that one day I would leave, and this seemed as good a time as any. While on the road, I applied for, and was offered, a temporary teaching position for the spring in New Jersey; when I arrived in New York City, I found a six-month sublet in Brooklyn, not far from where my very first apartment had been. A floor-through on the top floor of a three-story tenement building, it was a sweet sanctuary. In the littered back alley, beside the metal fire escape, a scraggly tree of heaven reached toward the sky. Once again, I felt as if I had come home. From my little perch, I taught two courses online and began the process of applying for a permanent teaching position in the New York area.

◆

I returned to a battered, nearly unrecognizable New Orleans for the first time in early November, accompanied by a friend from Minnesota who had offered to help. We were there to pack up my mother's apartment and to see what had become of my house. To my astonishment, I found it intact. The water had reached to within several inches of my flooring; some roof shingles had blown off and a gutter had come down. But the interior, as beautiful as ever, welcomed me: my desk, my bed, my dining-room table invited me to settle back in and resume my life. The butterfly garden I had exuberantly planted in the spring—neighbor children and I had watched delightedly as caterpillars glutted themselves, crafting fragile cocoons—was completely withered, with the exception of one sturdy milkweed stem; an orange and black monarch fluttered beside it. How could I think of leaving all this behind? There was still no gas service, but electricity had just returned to parts of the neighborhood. The street was largely deserted, but several neighbors were already back; it would be so simple just to stay.

As I met each old friend or neighbor in the nearly empty city, we looked deeply into each other's eyes. At first we didn't speak much, just gazed and held on to one another, aware of our good fortune in being alive, grateful to have found one another again. In our silence we acknowledged the unspeakable: the big one had come and gone, and we were still here. Others had not been so lucky.

I cried when I first saw again the man who had been cutting my lawn for two years; he had spent several days in the Convention Center and had seen things "people shouldn't see," as he told me. The waitress at the Palestinian restaurant, one of the first restaurants in the city to reopen, embraced me when I came in for some falafel. The plumber, the electrician, the air conditioning technician—all the men I called to help me get the house back in order—they each, miraculously, answered my calls, and when they arrived, we hugged. Everyone had a story, everyone needed to share it. The man who came to look at the damage on my roof told me of having rescued people in a boat. "You don't want to know what I saw," he said, even as he took out photographs. All these people were my comrades. How could I leave them?

But my mother was already settled in New York; my brother and I had found her an assisted-living facility in Brooklyn just beside Prospect Park; surely we couldn't move her again? She was nearly eighty-five and largely dependent on me. If she was to live in New York, then surely I should too. But *should* she live in New York? How could I know? I went to her apartment in Woldenberg Village, where I was overwhelmed by its beauty, entranced by the garden she had created during her three years there, by the lovely touches of color and grace in her rooms. Her neighbors surrounded me. "When will Nelly be back?" they asked. "Tell her we love her." As my friend and I painstakingly went through her things and made the choices of what to keep and what to discard, I could not stop crying. "Why are we doing this?" I kept asking. "Shouldn't we just both come back?" I called my mother. Was she sure she didn't want to return? "No," she said, firmly, "I don't want to go back."

A month later I returned to pack up *my* things. And again I wept, wondering what I was doing. Was it better to stay or to go? Was I abandoning my friends and colleagues in New Orleans? Was I running away from the hard work of reconstruction? I had always said that I wanted to go back to the East Coast, and wasn't this my opportunity? But what about my house, my job, my friends, the enchantment of this still-beautiful, fragile city? It was impossible to know the "right" thing. Was I making a real choice or was I compulsively reenacting the family drama—fleeing from a land that suddenly appeared dangerous and inhospitable? For as I had driven frantically northward, I had remembered my father's words, "There was no future for us there anymore. It wasn't safe."

Was there a future for me in New Orleans? How could I know? I had my house, but what about my job? Tenure at my university was in effect abolished, as financial exigency was declared. No one knew what cuts would be taken. Victorian literature was not a high priority, and I was not in the inner circle of decision makers. In New York, I might find more opportunity, more freedom. There was also the pleasure of familiarity, the ease of remembered people and places, the comfort of a culture I didn't have to struggle to interpret. Yet how could I say good-bye to all my friends in Louisiana? To the graceful, easy life I had established? On each visit my heart was wrenched; I understood at last why my mother never wanted to return to Cairo, did her best to forget it.

◆

Kay, with whom I managed to stay in touch in the aftermath of the storm, had evacuated to Illinois, to be with *her* friends and family. For the first few weeks she lived with her mother, then moved on to an apartment offered to her by friends of friends. We talked periodically, exchanging news, offering comfort. Her apartment in Mid-City, unlike my house, had not escaped. It had been flooded with two feet of water. Her grandmother's bed and dresser and night tables, her bookcases and books and rugs and chairs—everything was destroyed. What wasn't soaked in water was covered in mold. That glorious inheritance I had once coveted was gone, lost to the very forces I had once so cavalierly celebrated. But Kay and I both knew. "We had our precious lives," as Odysseus would say, and we had fared much better than many of our friends.

◆

After my semester in New Jersey, I found a job and an apartment in New York. The job is at a community college, teaching developmental writing, not Victorian literature. And the apartment is a studio, just one room in Brooklyn, not a three-bedroom house with a yard in New Orleans. None of the furniture I so painstakingly collected fits here. So I have spread it about, bequeathing my sofa to my mother, my dining-room table to a friend in New Jersey, my comfortable chairs to former neighbors in New Orleans. My high wooden bed, along with a rug and two small night tables, has found a place in a garret room of my brother's Catskill farmhouse, his underused weekend home that has become, in effect, my long-sought-for "grandmother's house." I go there whenever I can to sleep and to read and to dream—and to talk with the neighbors. Gordon Mulford, the man who lives just down the road, was born in the nineteenth-century farmhouse where I now arrange my books. His ninety-year-old mother, Elnora, who came to the house as a young bride, lives down the road in the other direction. She brings me peanut butter cookies, while I keep promising to make *ba'alawa*.

In Brooklyn I have my cats and my computer and a sofa bed, along with a new Persian rug that recalls those my mother brought with her from Cairo. Less than two weeks after I moved in, Medicine Hawk and Mary Ann came for a visit, along with Mary Ann's great-grandson Dylan. After three days of touring New York City, the four of us sat in a circle, cross-legged on my bare wooden floor in the ninety-five-degree heat. We invoked the four directions and smudged ourselves with sage, offering thanks for having come to this time and this place.

My apartment is two blocks from the assisted-living facility where my mother has made her new home and just down the street from the main branch of the Brooklyn Public Library. There is a fine coffee shop on the corner and the food co-op I belonged to nearly thirty years ago is a few blocks away. From my windows I can see the Statue of Liberty and the Empire State Building; I can watch the sun set over New York Harbor, and I occasionally see hawks circling overhead.

◆

For Rosh Hashanah, the new year 5768—September 2007—I prepare the apartment for the annual ritual. The new moon that brings in this new year is the same new moon that marks the beginning of Ramadan. I call Mervat in Washington to wish her a good holy month: *"Ramadan Mubarak,"* I say to her; *"L'Shana Tova,"* she says to me. In Brooklyn, we will be seven— my mother; my brother, Victor; my cousin Victor and his wife, Mary Linda; Colette, Suze's daughter; Colette's daughter and my goddaughter, Kiki; and me. I clean the house and think about the menu for days, even as I struggle to keep up with my classes. I settle on butternut squash and kale risotto; arugula and fennel salad; and spiced pear compote along with chocolate mousse for dessert. It is not at all what my mother would have made, but it's what I want just now. And of course there are the traditional foods she always served to symbolize renewal, triumph, good deeds, and sweetness for the coming year: the hard-boiled eggs and sliced apple with honey; the bright red pomegranates and tender *loubia* cooked with cinnamon and tomatoes; fresh dates and a leek omelet; and a new fruit—something we haven't yet eaten this season. I have found cactus pear—*figue de barbarie*—a fruit my mother remembers with joy from her Cairo childhood. There are fresh flowers throughout my tiny space and the table is set with an embroidered lace cloth. The silver is not polished, but it shines nevertheless with the beauty of our past, the promise of our future. When my family arrives, I am ready to lead the prayers with assurance, gratitude, and joy.

The view from here, Park Slope, Brooklyn, 2007.

Recipes   ◆   ◆   ◆

Stuffed Grape Leaves

(*Feuilles de vine* or *Wara anab*; Joyce's recipe)

- 1 lb. fresh or canned vine leaves
- 1 cup uncooked rice
- 2 bunches Italian parsley, chopped
- 1/2 cup dried chickpeas, soaked overnight
- 2 tomatoes, chopped
- 1/4 cup olive oil
- 1 cup lemon juice
- 3–4 cloves garlic, minced
- 2 teaspoon salt
- 1 teaspoon allspice
- 1 onion, finely chopped

1. Pour hot water over fresh vine leaves and set aside for 10 minutes. If the leaves are canned, drain, rinse, and soak in cool water 20 to 30 minutes. Drain and rinse again. Cut the stem off each leaf.

2. Press the soaked chickpeas under a rolling pin to remove the outer skin, then cook until tender (15–20 minutes).

3. Wash and drain the rice well. Combine with parsley, chickpeas, tomatoes, onions, and garlic. Add oil, lemon, salt, and allspice, and mix very well.

4. Place vine leaf on your work surface, underside up. Place 1 or 2 tablespoon of the filling on the leaf. Roll into a finger shape. When leaves have all been rolled, arrange the individual rolls in rows in a deep cooking pot. Sprinkle with salt. Place on top of the leaves a round flat plate and press lightly to prevent the rolls from loosening while cooking. Add just enough water to cover. Cook over low heat for 1/2 hour. Simmer another hour.

5. Remove and add more lemon juice if necessary. Unmold on a round shallow platter and garnish with tomatoes and boiled potato slices. Serve at room temperature.

Adapted from *Food for the Vegetarian: Traditional Lebanese Recipes* by Aida Karaoglan (New York: Interlink Books, 1987).

Stuffed Grape Leaves (Nelly's recipe)

- 1 lb. canned grape leaves
- 1/2 teaspoon salt
- 1/2 teaspoon allspice
- juice of 1 lemon
- 1 1/2 lbs. very lean chopped round beef
- 2 T white rice, washed well
- 1–2 tablespoon olive oil

1. Drain, rinse, and soak grape leaves in fresh water for 20 minutes. Drain and rinse again. Remove stem from each leaf.

2. Combine salt, allspice, lemon juice, beef, and rice. Mix well.

3. Place 1 tablespoon filling on each leaf, underside up, and roll into a tight, narrow cylinder.

4. Place olive oil in a heavy pot. Arrange rolls in rows in this pot. Cover with a heavy plate, placing stones on the plate if necessary, to ensure that rolls will not loosen.

5. Cover pot and place over very low heat. Allow leaves to "sweat"; once they have reabsorbed the steam, add a few additional tablespoons of lemon juice and water to cover. Cook over very low heat 1 to 1 1/2 hours. Let cool. Adjust seasoning and serve, warm or at room temperature.

Ful medammes

- 1 16 oz. can *ful* (fava beans, the small brown kind; best purchased from a Middle Eastern grocer. The large greenish fava
  beans will do in a pinch, but the small ones are best.)
- 2 just-boiled hard-boiled eggs, still warm
- olive oil
- juice of 1 or 2 lemons
- salt
- ground cumin

1. Heat the canned fava beans. Drain, reserving the liquid.
(You *could* prepare the beans "from scratch," beginning with
dried beans, soaking them overnight, and cooking them for 1
hour until tender. This of course is best, but we never did it at
home.)

2. Place the beans in a large bowl. Add 1 hard-boiled egg,
and mash the beans with the eggs, leaving some of the beans
intact, but creating a thick paste. Add some of the reserved
cooking liquid if desired.

3. Add seasonings to taste: perhaps 1 tablespoon oil, 2–3
T lemon juice, 1/2 teaspoon salt, 1/2 teaspoon cumin. Adjust
as necessary. (Need I say: we like it lemony, salty, generously
spiked with cumin.)

4. Garnish with slices of hard-boiled egg.

Ful medammes should be served immediately with warm pita
bread; *tahina*; and a "wilted" salad of lettuce, finely chopped
tomatoes, cucumbers, and scallions. The salad should be prepared the day before, seasoned with salt, lemon juice, olive oil,
and cumin. The lettuce leaves will have wilted and the cucumbers
and tomatoes will be soft. *Ful medammes* makes a good meal any
time of the day—breakfast, lunch, dinner. It is eaten everywhere
in Cairo and is served always with slightly different variations.
Be sure to have additional lemon juice, salt, and cumin on the
table so that individuals may adjust the seasoning to taste.

Tahina

- 1 cup tahini (ground sesame paste)
- 1/2 cup water
- 1/4 freshly squeezed lemon juice
- 1/2 teaspoon salt
- ground cumin
- ground garlic if desired

In a blender, combine tahini, water, and lemon juice. Blend until fully mixed. Pour into a bowl and add salt and cumin. Adjust lemon juice to taste. The tahina should not be as thick as hummus; it should be more like a liquidy dressing. To make hummus or baba ghanoush, simply add mashed chickpeas or roasted eggplant, mixing well.

Fila au fromage

- 6 eggs, beaten
- 1/2 lb. cottage cheese
- 4 oz. Parmesan cheese
- 1 lb. phyllo dough
- 1/2 lb. butter, melted

1. Combine eggs and cheese.

2. Working on a clean, flat surface, gently lay out one sheet of phyllo dough. Brush lightly with butter and fold lengthwise into thirds, making sure there is butter between each layer of dough. Brush with butter. Place a tablespoonful of the cheese mixture at one end of the strip and fold up the strip as you would a flag, creating a small triangular packet. Place the packet on a lightly buttered baking sheet. Continue in this manner until you have used all the phyllo and all the cheese mixture. Brush the tops of the phyllo packets with butter.

3. Bake at 350 degrees, 45 minutes to one hour, until golden and crisp.

Hamoud

- 1–2 tablespoon olive oil
- 3–4 cloves garlic, whole
- 2 large carrots, finely chopped
- 4 stalks celery, including the greens, finely chopped
- 2–3 small potatoes, peeled and diced
- 1/2 teaspoon salt
- 2–3 cups water
- juice of one or two lemons
- handful of dried mint, crushed

1. In a large, heavy saucepan, heat oil. Add garlic, carrots, celery, and potatoes. Toss vegetables to coat with oil. Sprinkle with salt, cover, and heat over medium heat until the vegetables begin to "sweat." Lower the heat, and simmer the vegetables in their own juices until softened. With a fork, gently mash some of the vegetables against the sides of the pot.

2. Add water and lemon juice. Bring to a boil and simmer gently for another 50 or 60 minutes until vegetables are very well cooked. Add mint. Adjust seasoning, adding lemon juice if necessary. Serve over rice and loubia.

Loubia

- 1–2 tablespoon olive oil
- 1 lb. fresh or frozen shelled black-eyed peas, preferably with some snaps
- 2 small tomatoes, cut into quarters
- 1/2–1 teaspoon salt
- 1 cinnamon stick

Heat olive oil in a medium saucepan. Add black-eyed peas, snaps, and tomatoes. Toss to coat with oil. Sprinkle with salt. Add cinnamon stick. Cover saucepan and heat over medium flame until the beans begin to "sweat." Lower heat and simmer gently, adding water only if necessary. Cook 30 to 40 minutes, until beans are very tender. Remove the cinnamon and serve.

Bamyia

- 1 tablespoon olive oil
- 1 lb. fresh okra, preferably very small and firm
- 3–4 cloves garlic, whole
- 2–4 tablespoon tomato paste
- 2 small fresh tomatoes, diced
- juice of 1 lemon
- 1 cup water

1. Wash and trim okra, cutting off the stems and removing the hard portions of the "cap" at the top of the vegetable. Be careful not to cut into the okra; if you do, your stew will be gummy—more like New Orleans gumbo than Egyptian *bamyia*. Pat the trimmed okra dry.

2. Heat olive oil in a heavy sauté pan. Add okra and brown well. Set aside.

3. In another pan, combine garlic, tomato paste, fresh tomatoes, lemon juice, and water. Stir well, and simmer for a few moments to create a sauce.

4. Add okra to the tomato sauce. Cover and simmer gently over low heat, 20–30 minutes, until the okra is tender. Do not stir while the okra is cooking.

Cousa be gebna

- 1 tablespoon olive oil
- 1 onion, diced
- 2 lbs. medium zucchinis, quartered lengthwise, scraped to remove seeds, then cubed
- 1/2 teaspoon salt
- 2 eggs, at room temperature
- 1/2 lb. small-curd cottage cheese, drained
- 1 cup grated Parmesan cheese
- 2 tablespoon crumbled feta

1. Sauté onion in olive oil until golden. Add zucchini. Toss to coat with oil. Sprinkle with salt and cook, covered, over medium heat until the zucchini begin to steam. Lower heat and simmer gently until zucchini is very soft, 20–30 minutes. Remove from heat, place zucchini and onion mixture in a bowl, and let cool to room temperature. The zucchini can be prepared in advance and refrigerated.

2. Beat eggs well. Stir in the cheeses. Combine this mixture with the cooled onions and zucchini. Spread in a 9-by-13-inch baking dish and bake at 350 degrees until the top is golden brown and bubbling, approximately 35 minutes.

Cousa be gebna was a family favorite, typically served with *m'ggadereh*, yogurt, and a tomato salad.

M'ggadereh

- 1 cup brown lentils
- 4 cup water
- 1 cup long grain white rice
- 1 large onion, sliced into thin rings
- 2 tablespoon olive oil
- 1/2 teaspoon salt, to taste

1. Combine lentils and 2 cups water in a saucepan. Bring to a boil, cover, and simmer gently 20 to 30 minutes, until lentils are beginning to soften. Add water as needed.

2. In a heavy frying pan, heat the oil. Add the onions, and over medium to high heat, fry them, stirring occasionally, until they are dark brown and very sweet. As the onions brown, turn the heat up to burn some of them until they are blackened and crisp. Drain the onions on paper towels.

3. When lentils are soft and most of the water is absorbed, add rice, salt, and the additional 2 cups of water. Stir well, adding 1/2 of the fried onions. Bring to a boil, cover, and simmer until the rice is done, another 20 to 30 minutes.

4. Top each serving of *m'ggaderah* with some of the reserved fried onions. Accompany with plain yogurt.

Tabbouleh

- 1 cup very fine bulgur
- 4 cups water
- 1–2 ripe tomatoes, very finely chopped
- 1 large cucumber, peeled and very finely chopped
- 1 bunch scallions, very finely chopped
- 1 bunch Italian parsley, with stems removed, very finely chopped
- 1–2 tablespoon olive oil
- juice of 1 or 2 lemons
- salt to taste
- ground cumin

1. Wash bulgur well and place in a large bowl with 4 cups of water. Allow to soak while you prepare the vegetables. It should soak for 30 to 60 minutes.

2. Combine tomatoes, cucumber, scallions, and parsley in a large bowl.

3. Drain the bulgur, using your hands to squeeze out excess water. Add to the chopped vegetables and mix well.

4. Add olive oil to the salad and mix well. Add lemon juice and salt to taste; season liberally with cumin. This salad, like the tomato salad, "ages" well; it's best after a few hours, and it keeps well for a day or two in the refrigerator.

Tomato Salad

- 3–4 large, ripe tomatoes
- 1 bunch Italian parsley
- 1 bunch fresh scallions
- juice of one or two lemons
- 2 tablespoons olive oil
- salt
- ground cumin

1. Wash tomatoes and cut into eighths. Place in a large glass bowl.

2. Wash parsley, remove stems, and chop leaves finely. Add to the tomatoes and mix well.

3. Wash scallions and slice into thin rounds, using the green tops as well as the white bulbs. Add to the tomatoes and mix.

4. Toss the tomatoes with the olive oil. Add fresh lemon juice to taste. Add salt and cumin—generously—to taste. (We like it very lemony, very salty, and with lots of cumin.)

This salad is best if allowed to sit at room temperature for several hours. The salt will draw the juices out of the tomatoes, and you will have a very liquid "dressing" that adds spice to the *m'ggadereh* or *cousa be gebna* with which the salad is typically served.

Charoseth

- 1 lb. small, pitted dates, chopped
- water
- 2 tablespoon sugar
- 1/2–1 cup red wine
- 1/4 cup matzoh crumbs
- 1/2 cup hazelnuts, roasted, peeled, and chopped
- 1/2 cup walnuts, chopped
- 1 teaspoon cinnamon

1. Simmer dates in a small amount of water until they are softened.

2. Transfer to a blender and chop.

3. Return mixture to a saucepan and bring to a boil, adding water if necessary. Add a tablespoon or two of sugar. Simmer gently for about 20 minutes, until the dates are completely soft and you have a thick puree.

4. Remove dates from heat and set aside, refrigerating until you are ready to serve.

5. Add wine, nuts, a handful of matzoh, and cinnamon to taste, creating a thick, crunchy "mortar."

Passover Nut Cake

- 7 eggs, separated
- pinch of cream of tartar
- 1/2 teaspoon cinnamon
- 1/2 teaspoon grated peel of mandarin orange
- 3/4 cup sugar
- 4 oz. chopped walnuts
- 4 tablespoon matzoh meal

1. Beat egg whites with cream of tartar until stiff. Do not let them dry out.

2. Beat egg yolks with cinnamon, orange peel, and sugar until thick. Stir in nuts and matzoh meal. Slowly fold in egg whites.

3. Pour into a baking dish. Bake at 350–375 degrees for 20 to 30 minutes until browned. Treat this cake as you would a soufflé; be careful not to bang things in the kitchen, and remove from oven gently. The cake should be airy and moist.

Ba'alawa

- 1 lb. sugar
- Juice of 1 lemon
- 1/2 teaspoon rosewater
- 1/2 teaspoon orangewater (also known as orange blossom water)
- 1 lb. shelled raw pistachios
- 1 lb. phyllo dough
- 3/4 lb. clarified sweet butter

1. Set aside 2–3 tablespoon of the sugar

2. In a heavy saucepan, slowly heat the remaining sugar until it becomes a slightly sticky, thick syrup. Add lemon juice and a bit of rosewater and orangewater to taste. Set aside to cool. Refrigerate.

3. Lightly grind pistachios. Mix in the reserved sugar, along with a small amount of butter. Mix well.

4. On a large, lightly buttered baking dish, spread a sheet of phyllo dough. Brush with butter. Spread another sheet. Brush with butter. Do this until you have used a little more than half of the dough. (You must work quickly to keep the dough from drying out. Keep unused dough under a damp towel.)

5. Pat the nut mixture onto the bottom layer of phyllo dough. Cover the mixture with additional sheets of dough, spreading butter between each sheet.

6. Using a sharp knife, cut the *ba'alawa* into lozenges. Pour remaining butter over the pastry.

7. Bake at 350 degrees until golden. Remove from oven and pour cold syrup over pastry. Allow to cool before serving.

Permissions

◆ ◆ ◆

The Feminist Press at The City University of New York is a nonprofit institution dedicated to publishing literary and educational works by and about women. We are the oldest continuing feminist publisher in the world; our existence is grounded in the knowledge that mainstream publishers seeking mass audiences often ignore important, pathbreaking works by women from the United States and throughout the world.

The Feminist Press was founded in 1970. In its early decades the Press launched the contemporary rediscovery of "lost" American women writers, and went on to diversify its list by publishing significant works by American women writers of color. More recently, the Press has added to its roster international women writers who are still far less likely to be translated than male writers. We also seek out nonfiction that explores contemporary issues affecting the lives of women around the world.

The Feminist Press has initiated two important long-term projects. Women Writing Africa is an unprecedented four-volume series that documents women's writing in Africa over thousands of years. The Women Writing Science project, funded by the National Science Foundation, celebrates the achievements of women scientists while frankly analyzing obstacles in their career paths. The series also promotes scientific literacy among the public at large, and encourages young women to choose careers in science.

Founded in an activist spirit, The Feminist Press is currently undertaking initiatives that will bring its books and educational resources to underserved populations, including community colleges, public high schools, literacy and ESL programs, and international libraries. As we move forward into the twenty-first century, we continue to expand our work to respond to women's silences wherever they are found.

For information about events and for a complete catalog of the Press's more than 300 books, please refer to our website: www.feministpress.org or call (212) 817-7926.